Understanding Virtual Universities

Roy Rada

intellect™
Bristol, UK
Portland, OR, USA

Hardback Edition First Published in Great Britain in 2001 by
Intellect Books, PO Box 862, Bristol BS99 1DE, UK

First Published in USA in 2001 by
Intellect Books, ISBS, 5824 N.E. Hassalo St, Portland, Oregon 97213-3644, USA

Editorial Consultant: Masoud Yazdani
Copy Editor: Holly Spradling
Production: Sally Ashworth, Robin Beecroft

A catalogue record for this book is available from the British Library

ISBN: 1-84150-052-6

Printed and bound in Great Britain by Cromwell Press, Wiltshire

Contents

Preface

Faculty and administrators in higher education *need* to convey clearly what they want information technology to do. Only after the appropriate models of education at various levels are adequately placed in the computer, can the computer help the people. Only faculty and administrators know what these models are.

Educational activities might be conveniently divided into levels relating to students, teachers, administrators, and society. However, these levels have critical interactions with one another. All faculty and administrators live through these interactions routinely but tend to under-appreciate that computer support for education must also work across all levels. This book emphasizes this integration as no other book does.

On the one hand, the book is a design for a particular kind of change. This change involves reaching students online and helping faculty and staff to manage the educational process. Technology-enhanced education can change relations among students, teachers, administrators, and society. Space, time, and organizational boundaries assume a different character. Faculty and administrators need to understand what can be done online and how the integration of levels of activity is vital to long-run impact.

On the other hand, the book reviews how technology might be used in universities. The range of tools and methods that are germane to the academy is wide. What tools are appropriate for what problems in higher education?

The *purpose* of this book is to help academics take advantage of information technology. The book analyzes key issues in the relationship between information technology tools and higher education. Readers will learn what has happened and what is likely to happen and should be better able to make decisions about directions to take on the information superhighway.

Contribution and Use

The *unique contribution* of this book is its integration of the issues facing faculty and administrators. What knowledge in the computer will support the work of the academy? What can information technology do with this knowledge? The history and current activities are reviewed in order to predict the direction to be taken over the next ten years.

Readers might use the knowledge gained from this book to improve higher education. For the teacher this may mean contributing to the growing body of electronic content for students. The teacher may also want to adopt new tools and methods for managing classes. The staff of the university should be better able to support the work of teachers and to create an information infrastructure and process for the university that helps students and teachers.

Audience

The intended *audience* is university academics whether involved in teaching directly or in the support of teaching. The reader needs no particular background knowledge. Readers from all disciplines – humanities, social sciences, natural sciences, engineering, and the professions – could benefit. Teachers might be expected to want to improve their teaching, and staff might be concerned with the broad impact of information technology on their part of the organization. Staff could come from all service units or any academic department.

In addition to the audience of faculty and staff in higher education, this book could serve audiences interested in higher education but outside the academy itself. Publishers and information technologists have clients in higher education. Concerned citizens, government officials, and employers should know the policy issues. Higher education is mandated by society to perpetuate the culture of that society, and in the end all members of society have a vested interest in how higher education works.

Knowledge Base and Author Experience

The *knowledge base* for this book includes the vast literature on the subject. Material from various journals, magazines, books, conference proceedings, newsletters, and reports are reflected in the chapters. Most importantly, the Web has become the source of information for this book.

The *author* has degrees in psychology, medicine, and computer science. His research has focused on educational technology, and his research publications on this topic are extensive. Furthermore, the author has served in various administrative capacities in higher education, to include titles as Virtual University Academic Officer, Co-Director of a Center for Distance Education, Director of an online Master's Degree, and director of a project on faculty empowerment through common tools. The author is also a columnist for one educational technology journal and editor of another.

What is Covered and What Not

The book covers individual students learning, groups in classrooms, universities as organizations, and emerging market forces:

- The chapter on individual learning relates theories of learning to content delivery and anticipates a strong, long-term future for intelligent, virtual reality tutoring systems.

- This chapter on learning is followed by a chapter on teaching and the classroom. The new classroom will increasingly help students and teachers promote person-to-person mediated interactivity.

- The chapter on universities concerns the delivery of degrees. Models of universities are advanced and related to the information technology that supports them. Quality control can be further supported in online universities.

- The chapter on new markets focuses on the evolving marketplace, as reflected in employers of companies and brokers, such as publishers.

Each chapter calls for refined and extended models that are broadly accepted across the academy. Such models might also be called standards and support the development of information technology applications in education. The reader should see that ultimately the models must integrate individual learning, classroom teaching, and school administration.

This book focuses on higher education. While training can be included under the heading of education, this book pays much less attention to skill-based training than to concept-oriented education. The book is relevant to education at the elementary, middle, and high school level, but the peculiar needs of kindergarten through high school education are not studied. This book is not intended as a thorough review of the relevant disciplines, such as computer science or pedagogy. Nor is a survey of existing commercial tools offered. Rather the book is intended to help people appreciate the importance of clear models and the interactions among levels.

Acknowledgements

For the opportunity to explore the use of information technology in higher education the author owes an enormous debt to many in academia. The author's thanks go first to the colleagues and students who have worked with him in applying the new tools. Those leaders who have allowed him some responsibilities in these matters include then Provost Tom George of Washington State University, WA, USA, Dean Susan Merritt of Pace University, NY, USA, and numerous administrators and faculty of the University of Maryland, Baltimore County, MD, USA. The

Board of Directors of the Globewide Network Academy has provided a constant source of lively debate about the future of higher education and the Web. Finally, the author's deepest appreciation goes to his three children, wife, and parents whose physical presence has no substitute in the online world.

Roy Rada, M.D., Ph.D.

Roy's desktop and Roy

Introduction

University education is important to the *long-term viability* of society. The information superhighway or cyberspace is changing society. How should education respond to this changing environment?

Education in Cyberspace

The Internet is enabling a new way of life called 'the Web lifestyle'. Because the Internet is a worldwide communications infrastructure that depends on electricity, its popular acceptance is an extension of the 'electricity lifestyle'. The Web lifestyle, like the electricity lifestyle, is characterized by rapid innovations in applications.

The Web lifestyle will increasingly equalize opportunities for skilled people around the world. If one had to guess someone else's approximate income today and were limited to a single polite question, one might ask for the country of residence. The reason is the huge disparity in average wages from country to country. In twenty years, to guess somebody's income, the most telling question may be: "What's your education?" In a Web-enabled society, some people can participate in some activities from anywhere that is connected to the Web. Gifted computer programmers in India with adequate Web access can contribute as well to a software development company in California, USA as could programmers living in California.

Information technology could empower teachers and students more than any other group of

Figure 1: "Individual, Group, and Organization". The individual learner with a tool to help explore information, the group studying information together with the help of a laptop, and the school housing cohorts of students – these three connect one to the other in a never-ending cycle of learning.

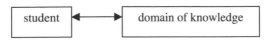

Figure 2: "Student". The student interacts with a domain of knowledge.

knowledge workers. Teacher involvement is a necessity. A connected university can become the basis for a connected learning society that encourages lifelong learning for all citizens.

What, more precisely, are the opportunities for higher education to exploit the Internet? Consider individuals, groups, and organizations in terms of the student learning from courseware, the teacher with a class, and the school with its degree programs (see Figure 1 "Individual, Group, and School"). What are the challenges in terms of people and technology in each of these categories?

The electronic book and the online multiple-choice question are commonplace. What will come next? Will individual faculty produce brilliant, new electronic products that guide a student to learning without further teacher intervention? Will universities form new units that support the development of this electronic content?

The classroom is a special social process for teachers and their students. When the teacher-student interaction goes online, how does the teacher manage the new social process? Does the teacher simply digitize lectures and respond to email questions? Now when students interact with one another, their transactions are also logged on the computer. Can teachers guide these student-student interactions in a useful way?

Without a formal school, the situation for university teachers and students would be more primitive than it was in the Middle Ages. Modern society relies on universities to provide cohesive curricula and to be responsible for quality control. The student wants not an individual class but a degree and the cohesiveness of the courses within the degree. To what extent will schools become paperless and rely on online information? What technical, conceptual, financial, and other issues influence the adoption of information technology by universities?

Changes at the level of universities cannot be effectively considered without considering the environment in which the universities exist. One important component of this environment is employers whose employees the universities educate. The information superhighway can bring together employers and universities in new ways. Are there examples of alliances on the Internet of universities and companies? What role will organizations like publishers play in the evolving marketplace of higher education?

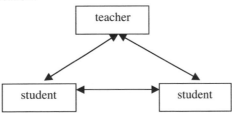

Figure 3: "Classroom". The teacher guides students.

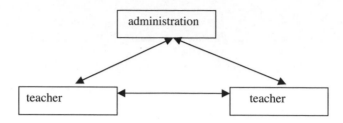

Figure 4: "University". The administration guides teachers.

The many questions to be addressed in the coming chapters all lead to the one grand question of how higher education will use information technology. One answer is that the best fit of technology to the university depends on the specifics of who is to use the technology and for what purpose. A rich map of people, problems, and tools needs to be developed and continually extended as the people, problems, and tools change. This book will present the beginnings of this map, as it lays out the major landmarks that are currently recognized. Readers will hopefully be able to find new points to put on the map as the reader explores the world of universities and education at the speed of thought.

Integration across Levels

The claims of this book are that:

1. a clear understanding of the structure and function in a particular higher education activity lends the activity to computer-support and
2. the strength of computer-support for any particular activity ultimately depends on the connectivity among the activities.

As already noted, broadly speaking, the chapters of the book correspond to students, teachers, administrators, and society. At each level the claim is that quality control can be semi-automated when the educational activities are understood and adequately modeled inside the computer:

- Within the realm of the individual learning, the computer must model the interaction between the student and the domain of knowledge so as to know when to intervene and provide guidance (see Figure 2 "Student").

- For the teacher, the computer should model the student-teacher interaction and student-student interaction so that the computer can support quality control over these interactions (see Figure 3 "Classroom").

- Administrators want to model the teacher-administrator and teacher-teacher interactions and offer support where most needed (see Figure 4 "University").

- Finally the society wants to keep track of what the schools are doing internally and how they relate to one another (see Figure 5 "Society").

These four components of student, teacher, administrator, and society have various relations to one another. In one simplification, the society guides the administrators, who guide the teachers, who guide the students, who in turn guide the society by representing the needs of the future (see

Figure 6 "Cycle of Students, Society, Administrators, and Teachers"). One could also picture various flows of money and of documents from entity to entity.

Most important to understand is that successful computer support at any one level ultimately requires profound interaction with the other levels. The student-content interaction is influenced by many factors. Students learn from content that publishers produce, i.e. coming from the entity called 'society' in the Figure 6 "Cycle of Students, Society, Administrators, and Teachers." Likewise coming from the 'society' level are the employers and families that support students financially and morally. The student history must be modeled before the computer could well know what kinds of interventions are appropriate, and this student history knowledge would come from the 'school' level.

The teacher in interacting with students at the 'classroom' level needs a model of the content that the students are studying in order to appreciate what the student-teacher and student-student interactions signify relative to mastering the domain knowledge. The grading that the teacher does significantly influences student motivation but this grading is set within the context of the school and how other teachers grade. For an online classroom, simple things like a student roster should not have to be manually created by the teacher but should be automatically imported to the online classroom from the university student registration system.

The school provides graduation rules for students to follow but must be sensitive to what society wants of graduated students for otherwise the school risks setting the wrong rules. In anticipating enrollments and recruiting faculty to teach courses, the administration needs to be in close contact with employers who are paying student tuition costs to attend certain types of courses. Different universities should collaborate with one another to assure the appropriate breadth and depth of educational offerings across institutions.

The Culture of Universities

Some academics claim that universities will change radically due to information technology (Noam, 1995). However, entrepreneur Gates (1999) notes that, while education is an area in which the Web life style would seem to hold most promise, the rate of change there has not been as great as in some other sectors of society. Education is unfortunately limited by adequate funding.

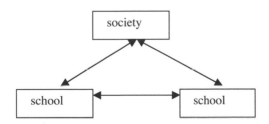

Figure 5: "Society". Society guides the schools.

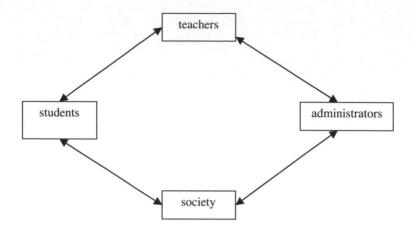

Figure 6: "Cycle of Students, Society, Administrators, and Teachers".
The relations of people who in turn provide the needs that guide the future
development of 'society'.

Analyses of the deployment of technology in universities have tended to note its failure to affect the day-to-day values and practices of many teachers and administrators. This is generally regarded as an implementation failure, or as resulting from some shortcoming on the part of teachers or technologists. Such a construction is predicated on the assumption that the refused technology is value-free. However, technology is not value-free. The failures of technology to alter the look-and-feel of universities frequently result from a mismatch between the values of universities and those values that are embedded within the technology itself.

For nearly a century, outsiders have been trying to introduce technologies into universities. After proclaiming the potential of the new tools to usher in an age of efficiency and enlightenment, technologists find to their dismay that teachers can often be persuaded to use the new tools only slightly, if at all. Hodas (1996) says:

> What is often overlooked in such assessments, however, is that schools themselves are a technology, by which I mean a way of knowing and acting applied to a specific goal, albeit a technology so familiar that it has become transparent. Schools are intentional systems for preserving and transmitting information…and have evolved and been refined over many years. Since their form has remained essentially unchanged over this time, we can even say that they have been optimized for the job we entrust to them, that over time the technology of schooling has been tuned. When schools are called upon to perform more 'efficiently', to maximize outputs of whatever type…it is their capacity to act as technologies, as rational institutions, that is being called upon.

Universities are not a simple technology. They have multiple purposes and identities. Considering the culture of a university is critical to understanding the university's relation to information technology. Indeed for all organizations this relationship between culture and tools is vital (Orlikowski, 1992).

Universities face many internal and external forces (Zammuto, 1982). Public universities and their employees have historically been exempt from many forms of pressure that can be brought to bear on organizations from without. Successful change in the university must be consistent with the values of the teachers and administrators and must be perceived as supporting the cultural mission to which the members of the organization subscribe.

The use of information technology in universities can only be expected to change when the people who are expected to change are comfortable with the change. Understanding the strengths and weaknesses or the costs and benefits of various information technology tools is thus just one of the factors in change for universities. The ensuing chapters will describe various advances in technology and their application in higher education. The special needs of students, faculty, and staff are emphasized (Snyder, 1995). The suggestion is not that information technology should be widely or quickly adopted. Rather readers are asked to examine the activities of the university and to identify where these activities can be precisely described and supported by a computer.

Learning and Content

In this chapter readers will explore:

- the complex mapping among students, the tools and methods used for learning, and the learning problems,

- the different types of learning as reflected in the taxonomy of learning types,

- the impact of learning by doing,

- the impact of different media on different learning objectives,

- the history of intelligent tutoring systems,

- the components of intelligent tutoring systems,

- standards for content,

- examples and patterns of content production in higher education institutions, and

- the extensive organizational commitment required for content production.

Figure 7: Student at the workplace studying for an online course.

Introduction

Under what conditions does learning occur? The dream of digital content developers is that students can interact with computers in ways that would have otherwise been restricted to the interaction between students and teachers. Since at least the 1960s some educators have been attracted to the possibilities of using computers and networks to support learning. Have the anticipated impacts followed the expectations of the enthusiasts?

The efforts to apply computers and networks to learning have been so many and so diverse that the terminology that applies is also varied. At the level of an individual student learning online, some of the terms that have been applied to the technology include: courseware, learning technology systems, computer-based training systems, electronic performance support systems, computer-assisted instruction systems, intelligent tutoring systems, education and training technology, Web-based instruction systems, and interactive learning environments. In this chapter the preferred synonym will be 'courseware' and refers to the content plus technology that is used to support individual learning.

People have a long history across generations of dealing effectively with paper forms of information. Should paper be replaced with computer forms? Or might the better solution be complementary combinations of paper and digital media?

A wide range of tools is available to educators, but what experience has been gained in the application to learning. Unfortunately, the wealth of experience does not distill easily into detailed guidance about what to do next. The many developments in the field have often been one without proper reference to another. Even the terminology used by the developers has not been consistent. Thus comparing one observation to another observation is fraught with difficulties of knowing whether one person's apples are the same as another person's apples or whether apples are instead being compared to oranges. How will agreement arise about what has been done?

Learning and Pedagogy

Some psychologists specialize in learning psychology; some educators specialize in pedagogy or the art of teaching. What is known about *learning and teaching*?

Taxonomy of Learning Types

A group of educational psychologists developed a classification of levels of learning. This became taxonomy, sometimes called *Bloom's taxonomy* that included three overlapping domains: the cognitive, affective, and psychomotor (DLRN, 1997 and Bloom, 1956).

Cognitive learning is demonstrated by knowledge recall and the intellectual skills: Bloom's taxonomy identified six levels within the cognitive domain, from the simple recall or recognition of facts, at the lowest level, through increasingly more complex and abstract mental levels, to evaluation at the highest level.

For a teacher to help a student integrate new knowledge into the student's existing models of the self or the environment, the teacher must help the student identify the relationships between what the student already knows and what is new to be learned. Giving students questions to answer that stretch their thinking about the new knowledge typically does this. Below are the six cognitive levels as they correspond to questions that a teacher might ask to help a student learn:

- *Knowledge* involves recall of information and relates to questions such as whom, what, when, where, how...?

- *Comprehension* involves organizing and selecting facts and ideas, and asks how would you describe in your own words?

- *Application* is problem solving or use of facts, rules and principles. Typical questions take the form: How is...an example of...? How is...related to...?

- *Analysis* is separation of a whole into component parts. Questions include: What are the parts or features of...? How does... contrast with...?

- *Synthesis* is the combination of ideas to form a new whole. Questions include: What would you predict from...? How would you create a new...?

- *Evaluation* is the development of opinions, judgments or decisions. Typical questions are: What is the most important...? What criteria would you use to assess...?

Affective learning is demonstrated by behaviors indicating attitudes of awareness, interest, attention, concern, and responsibility and ability to listen and respond in interactions with others. The depth and breadth of information processed and what and how much is learned and remembered is influenced by

- self-awareness and beliefs about self and one's learning ability (personal control, competence and ability);

- clarity and saliency of personal goals;

- personal expectations for success or failure;

- affect, emotion and general states of mind; and

- the resulting motivation to learn.

Psychomotor learning is demonstrated by grace and actions which demonstrate the motor skills such as use of precision instruments or tools.

Basic principles of learning motivation and effective instruction apply to all groups of learners. However, learners differ in their preferences for learning mode and strategies, the pace at which they learn, and unique capabilities in particular areas. These differences are a function of both *environment and heredity*.

Learning by Doing

Some say that students will learn better when they can test the models they are learning in real-world situations. Educators who are also proponents of using the computer in education sometimes claim that *learning by doing* is vital and that computers can support this. This approach is also called constructivist learning (Jonassen, 2000).

Roger Schank directs the Institute for the Learning Sciences at Northwestern University, Illinois, USA. Schank (1997, 2000) claims that the number one problem with education is:

> Schools act as if learning can be dissociated from doing. There really is *no learning without doing*.

Learning by doing can be realized in any discipline. For instance, students can explore the history of the American Civil War by constructing an economic model of factors motivating the North and the South. Such a learning-by-doing approach contrasts with an approach in which students are asked to read a chapter about the American Civil War and then to answer multiple-choice questions about the dates at which certain events occurred. The constructivist approach addresses a higher level of learning than does the memorization approach.

Pedagogy

Ben Shneiderman's (1997) motto is 'Real Projects for Real People'. He says (Shneiderman, 1993):

> The post-TV media of computers and communications enables teachers, students, and parents to creatively develop education by engagement and construction. Students should be given the chance to engage with each other in team projects, with the goal of constructing a product that is useful or interesting to someone other than the teacher. Challenges remain such as scaling up from small class projects to lecture sections with hundreds of students, covering the curriculum that is currently required by many schools, evaluating performance, and assigning grades.

Students will be engaged by writing and drawing, composing and designing, and planning and drawing. Teachers should promote engaging in the world, helping where needed, caring for others, and communicating ideas. Project-oriented learning allows the aforementioned guidelines to be realized in the most natural way.

In project-oriented learning or learning-by-doing, students need to have objectives and to be assessed for their progress towards the objectives. Educators should monitor the following stages of the *education cycle* (see Figure 8 "Education Cycle"):

1) identify and analyze education needs or objectives,

2) design and plan education,

3) provide and deliver education, and

4) evaluate education outcomes and improve the education process.

In the ideal situation, the output of one stage will provide the input for the succeeding stage.

Identifying and analyzing needs is the starting point. Educators should identify the needs for students, assess the competencies of the students, and develop plans to close any gaps. The *design and plan* phase provides the specifications for the education. This phase includes:

- the design and plan of actions to address the needs identified in the earlier process; and

- the design of the criteria for evaluating the outcomes and monitoring the education process.

The relevant methods of education that can meet the education needs should be identified. This cycle of identify, plan, deliver, and evaluate makes sense for teaching and for other activities too.

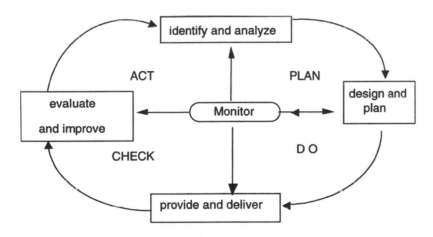

Figure 8: Education Cycle. Education should begin with an identified need. The education is then planned, delivered, and finally the impact is evaluated.

Delivering Interactive Content

Simply delivering information by computer has relatively little advantage over delivering by paper in many cases. However, with the computer one can gain *interactivity* that is not possible with paper. By placing some intelligence into the computer so that the interactions it provides do some work of a teacher, one gains a kind of cost effectiveness in education. Much work has been done over the past forty years to help establish the principles and practice by which computers can incorporate some of the intelligence of the teacher (Wenger, 1987; Cartwright, 1993).

Historical Snapshot

One example of courseware incorporating multiple techniques for delivery and interaction is described next. This example was ahead of its time but illustrates the kind of product that has appeared in isolation repeatedly in the past. Such products may someday become prevalent in educational environments and the ensuing sections sketch how such products might appear.

This example from the 1980s integrates several tools and methods. In 1985 (Diaz 1991) students taking the course *Introductory Pathology* at Cornell School of Medicine, New York, USA, could enroll in PathMac, an electronic version of the course. Macintosh computers tied into the PathMac database were scattered throughout the campus for student access. Students could study online textbooks, run simulated laboratories, or test their mastery of physiology via online dissections. PathMac provided online access to approximately seven gigabytes of images and bibliographical material that could be searched intelligently, cross-referenced, and printed.

One online application was an electronic pathology text called *HyperPath*, which included large portions of a version of a well-known textbook. Teachers could add text and graphics. A visual archive called Carousel included thousands of images. Carousel images could be paired with questions.

Another program was used to perform *simulated laboratory experiments* that otherwise would be performed on live cats. The system could test the effect of various drugs on simulated cat muscle. The students chose which drug to inject, in what quantity, and then electrically stimulated the muscle and recorded the results on a simulated strip chart. Much more control over the results could be achieved than is possible with live muscle.

Medical students can explore patient treatment situations through simulation. For instance, in one simulation a young man presents with a severe asthmatic attack after a walk (Corvetta et al. 1991). The season is spring and the walk was in the countryside, both facts suggesting an allergic etiology of the disease. If the student's choice is to perform a case history or skin tests, the computerized tutor comments that the choice is wrong and that the priority is to relieve the patient's symptoms. A physical examination and appropriate treatment should be immediately performed. Once the prescription of the correct medication results in normalization of the respiratory sound and congratulations from the tutor, a case history may be taken. The tutor emphasizes the key questions in the case history that should be asked in order to determine the possible allergic origin of a respiratory disease. Next the student performs the skin tests and evaluates the reactions. Diagnosis of the allergy pollens may be made and a correct hyposensitizing treatment planned. Such simulations can be part of an effective learning environment.

Multiple-choice Questions

The preceding Pathmac example did not have widespread impact on the teaching in medical schools. However, multiple-choice questions delivered online have had a major impact on teaching in medical schools and elsewhere. The computer is an excellent tool for supporting multiple-choice questions or tests. The user chooses a particular answer and the computer can immediately explain to the student whether the student's answer was correct or incorrect. By storing explanations for why an answer is incorrect, the computer can also readily supply this explanation to the user. Multiple-choice questions have been a mainstay of interaction for courseware for decades.

Multiple-choice tests have been shown to promote retention learning. However, announcements of an upcoming test did not have a positive effect on retention learning without a test actually being given. Increased studying due to anticipation of a test did not result in better retention – only the act of taking the test increased retention (Haynie, 1994).

In a multiple-choice question, students must select the correct answer from a number of possible answers. The incorrect answers are termed distracters (see Figure 9 "Multiple Choice Question"). These distracters should embody misconceptions; partly correct answers and common errors of fact or reasoning so that they distract students who are not well-prepared for the test from giving the correct answer.

Multiple-choice questions are usually used to test a student's ability to recall information, to interpret data or diagrams, and to analyze and evaluate material. The principal strengths of multiple-choice tests are (Ballatyne, 2000):

- They test a wide range of issues in a short time.

- A computer can reliably mark them, as all answers are predetermined.

- Computer marking gives easy access to an item analysis of questions to pinpoint problem areas for students.

- A large bank of questions can be built up to reduce future preparation time.

- They can be used for quick revision at the start or end of a class.

The principal weaknesses of multiple-choice question tests are:

- They do not test a student's ability to develop and organize ideas and present these in a coherent argument.

- It takes a long time to write plausible distracters - especially in cases where higher order cognitive skills are being tested.

- Restrictions are placed on a students' answers, as they must select from the author's alternatives.

- Questions are often re-used which means attention to security.

- Questions need to be pre-tested and items reviewed to ensure the validity of the items.

Other possible disadvantages to online multiple-choice questions are the same as the disadvantages that can accrue for any computer use, namely, that certain groups of people do not have as ready access to or familiarity with computers (Fairtest, 2000).

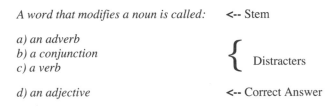

Figure 9: "Multiple-Choice Question". In this standard form of a multiple choice question the stem is the question. The options are listed underneath the question. Distracters are incorrect but plausible options.

Despite some unresolved problems, online quizzes can be useful. Students at the University of California at Irvine's Graduate School of Management, California, USA, carry their laptops into classrooms in which every seat has a high-speed Internet connection. Teachers give Web-based electronic quizzes at the start of class, receive instant feedback on how the students did on each question, and adjust their lecture plans on the spot to focus on the areas where students need the most help.

Less than a second after finishing each test the students can see all wrong answers on their screens and an explanation of what the right answer should have been. This instant feedback, according to the school's Administrative Computing Manager Tony Zamanian, has changed the way the school uses tests and quizzes. Zamanian says (QuestionMark, 2000):

> The tests are not only tests any more; rather they are tools that help students understand what is required of them. Faculty members can convey to students the kind of information they want to receive from them. We are starting to look at tests as learning tools in a very active sense of the word; instant feedback gives students an idea of their strengths and weaknesses and puts them on the right track for studying the material.

Public Policy Professor Peter Navarro says that students thrive on the instant feedback they receive from computer-based tests. Navarro sees the primary goal of such tests as motivation rather than evaluation:

> The ability to administer electronic tests gives me a very powerful tool to encourage students to keep up with the reading material on a regular basis. I believe such even-paced learning greatly increases the half-life of a student's knowledge retention relative to the 'cram before exam' mode that so many students fall into.

Electronic testing can be a complement to rather than a substitute for other forms of testing and interaction between teacher and student.

In addition to being used by teachers as learning aids, online multiple-choice tests are also increasingly used for large-scale, standardized testing. The Educational Testing Service (ETS), in the USA, for example, introduced its computerized Graduate Record Exam in October 1992. ETS's Graduate Management Admission Test was computerized in 1993 and delivered to over one million candidates in 1999 alone. Computerized tests are also part of ETS's teacher tests, and the National Council Licensure Examination, USA for nurses is only available on computer. In addition, many colleges, universities, and school districts are using computerized placement tests.

Directions in Testing

Most multiple-choice tests are premised on a psychological model that probably owes more to the behaviorism of the first half of the twentieth century than to the cognitive science of the second half. The new generation of electronic tests incorporate advances in technology, psychometrics, and to a growing extent, cognitive science (Bennett, 2000).

Widespread change has come first in the nature of test questions and the formats for response, and the possibilities both provide for measuring new skills. In conventional testing, audio or video was used only when a critical skill could not be adequately assessed by standard methods (e.g., when measuring foreign language listening skills). However, the widespread accessibility of multimedia computers supports incorporating sound and video. For example, many introductory college history courses include the analysis of artifacts. To reflect this emphasis, quizzes in history should ask students to use artifacts (e.g., excerpts from diaries, news articles, letters, maps, and political cartoons) as evidence to formulate a response to a question prompt. Twentieth-century history is documented by film and broadcasts, as well as by print. Computers can accommodate all the artifacts used on the conventional test as well as historical films, TV, and radio broadcasts, thereby extending the range of source material with which students must be proficient.

While multimedia is used to extend measurement of traditional skills, it can also be used to measure new skills. Questions often assess skill in getting information from print because reading is considered critical to success in school, in most jobs, and in activities of daily living. However, electronic media have become very important in communicating information. For instance, most Americans get their news from TV. Consequently, students should be able to process information from a variety of sources. Given this expectation, tests should evaluate not only how effectively people handle print but also how well they reason with information from film, radio, TV, and computers.

To help create and calibrate items at the required rate, new tools allow developers to construct question templates or select them from large libraries and then vary both surface elements tangential to the solution as well as deeper structural elements. Item generation tools may also eventually help in specifying test designs – the type, organization, number, and parameters of tasks needed to achieve a specific result. Once a test design is specified, these tools could automatically suggest which question templates to use. A variety of standard designs derived from cognitive principles might exist from which the developer could select or create a new design, thereby pushing tests toward formulations based more solidly on cognitive theory.

The new generation of tests combines advances in psychometrics with technology to deliver tests adaptively. The computer selects questions based in part on previous responses, tailoring the test to individual skill levels. Trends in interaction between student and teacher will include increased intelligence in the computer and virtual reality. With intelligent tutoring systems, students' knowledge will be dynamically modeled using cognitive and statistical approaches capable both of guiding instruction on a highly detailed level and of providing a general summary of overall standing. Instruction will be adapted not only to the multiple dimensions that characterize standing in a broad skill area, but to personal interests and background, allowing more meaningful accommodation to diversity than was possible with earlier approaches. Simple multimedia exercises will give way to virtual reality simulations. These simulations will model complex environments, such as science labs, and give students a chance to learn and be assessed under conditions similar to those encountered by practitioners. Details about intelligent tutoring and virtual reality come in the next sections.

Intelligent Tutors

A computer system that emulates the expertise of a tutor is called an intelligent tutoring system. Intelligent tutoring systems have an architecture that can be viewed as including an expert or domain module, a student module, and an instructional or pedagogical module (Vasandani and Govindaraj, 1995; Murray, 1999). The domain module contains the domain expertise which is also the knowledge to be taught to the student. The student module contains a model of a student's current level of competence. The pedagogy module is designed to sequence instructions and tasks based on the information provided by the domain and student models. The three modules together interact with the learner.

The *student module* in an intelligent tutoring system maintains a model of the student's current understanding of the domain. It stores actions taken by the student and has some means of representing the student's knowledge derived from recorded actions. Representation of data in such a student model must facilitate its comparison with the domain model of the task to enable evaluation of misconceptions in the student (Van Marcke, 1995).

The *pedagogy module* of an intelligent tutoring system is responsible for several activities. Its primary function is to control the curriculum, that is, select the material to be presented and its form of presentation. In addition, the pedagogy module evaluates students' misconceptions based on observed actions. The pedagogy module makes use of rules pertaining to presentation methods, query response, and conditions for tutorial intervention.

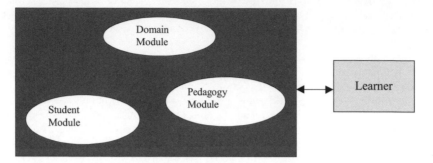

Figure 10: "Intelligent Tutoring System and Learner". The student, domain, and pedagogy modules are connected to the learner.

An intelligent tutoring system models students' understanding of a topic as they progress through tasks, and compares this against a model of what an expert in that domain understands. If there is a mismatch, it can use its domain model to generate an *explanation* in that domain that will help the student understand. Broad actions considered by the pedagogy module include:

- Give help,
- Motivate learners,
- Give exercise,
- Guide with explanation, and
- Assess student progress.

As evidenced from an extract of taxonomy of intelligent tutoring systems (Mizoguchi et al. 1996), the interactions between the tutoring system and the learner must specify the mode of interaction, communication roles, and content type (see Figure 11 "Learner-system Interactions").

The *WEST courseware system* is well-documented in the literature. It selects and presents a problem to students (Brown and Burton, 1978). Based on the student response, WEST updates its student model and determines whether students have mastered the problem or not. If WEST knows a better rule for solving the problem than the student seems to have invoked, then WEST presents the superior rule to the student along with an explanation.

Given the great effort required to build an intelligent tutoring system, one question naturally arises as to the extent to which computers can be programmed to build on its experiences so as to improve the domain, pedagogy, or student modules. Machine learning is relevant to intelligent tutoring in multiple ways. For one, we are trying to help students learn and we might expect that insights about machine learning and human learning would be cross-fertilizing. Also an intelligent tutoring system that had a machine-learning component might improve its ability to deal effectively with different students. In one model of a learning system the *environment* supplies information to a *performance element* that uses a knowledge base to perform its task (Forysth and Rada, 1986). A learning element uses this information to make improvements in the knowledge base (see Figure 12: "Learning System"). To extend this model, the environment is seen as providing student interactions and the performance element decides what pedagogical material to present next to the student. Based on the environmental feedback to the performance element, the learning element operates on the knowledge base so as to produce better knowledge.

```
Learner-system interaction

Mode of interaction
 Menu
 Text
 Speech
 Virtual reality
Communication roles
 Teacher-Learner
 Master-Apprentice
 Collaborative partners
Content types
 Problem
 Question
 Example
Control
 In-turn
 Free dialogue
 Case-oriented
```

Figure 11: Learner-system Interactions. A part of the taxonomy with just 3 bottom-level children.

Virtual Reality Tutors

For students to learn effectively, students must feel engaged, and tutors can increase that sense of engagement with the appropriate use of *media* and of simulations that involve the media. Multimedia engages students through communication channels. Virtual reality enables the real world to be simulated and manipulated in realistic ways without, necessarily, the danger, inconvenience, or cost consequences of action in the real world. An early example of artificially representing the world is flight simulation used for training pilots. Computer-generated graphics rather than actual video often provide the visual aspect of the virtual reality world. Users know that the virtual reality world is simulated but can accept its objects such as landscapes, rooms and corridors as representations of the real world. Some tactile sensation is also offered by the use of touch sensitive pressure pads. Hand gloves may be used to manipulate objects in this way. Movement in this artificial world is commonly synchronized with the user's actual bodily movements of walking, jumping, and running. The *virtual environment* can be defined as a multi-dimensional experience that is totally or partially computer-generated and can be accepted as cognitively valid (Jense and Kuijper, 1993).

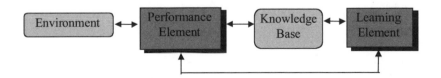

Figure 12: Learning System. The environment is the basis for performance feedback to refine the knowledge base.

Trainee surgeons may acquire some of the skills required to perform *keyhole surgery* by practicing on virtual patients. Keyhole surgery is already performed remotely, by means of microscopic cameras, which can be connected to monitors displaying close-up images of the patient's tissue. The keyhole method of surgery is beneficial to patients in terms of minimizing surgical intervention and improving recovery rates but it is difficult to teach. Real patients may not be used for practice. A virtual reality patient displayed on the monitor can, however, provide a good simulation, enabling the surgeon to learn the required techniques by doing surgery.

A virtual reality tutoring system for mechanical engineering could immerse students inside a three-dimensional setting derived from a ship's engine room (Stiles et al. 1996). One or more students, each with an associated viewer, are in this ship's engine room environment (see Figure 13 "Virtual Reality Environment"). Objects in the environment, such as control systems, actuators, and other equipment, are simulated. Other team members, or an instructor, are also simulated. As students select and manipulate objects in the virtual environment, they cause simulations to change the state of the world, and these changes are sensed by *agent systems*, which can intervene, explain, or demonstrate tasks for the student. The changes caused by the student, the objects being simulated, and the computer manages all the agents representing other people.

Figure 13: Virtual Reality Environment. The screen from Virtual Reality Tutor (Stiles et al. 1996) is part of what students see.

The costs of developing an intelligent tutoring system are high. The *costs* of developing an intelligent virtual reality tutoring system are even higher. The examples given of successful applications in shipboard engine maintenance and keyhole surgery are examples where the costs of traditional education are very high. The expense of the intelligent virtual reality tutor is born by the organization that otherwise has to pay for the regular teachers and equipment.

With larger audiences, the *per student cost* of a virtual reality tutor declines. A science class may not be expensive to teach to a few students, and thus the school is not willing to spend millions to have a virtual reality tutor. However, given that many students every day are studying science, the cost of a successful intelligent virtual reality tutoring system could cost millions of dollars to develop but still cost only a few dollars on a per student basis. However, another challenge is whether students will have access to the necessary computers to run the system. As the technological infrastructure of the society continues to advance, the extent to which students will have equipment that supports virtual reality systems will increase.

Meta-analysis

Many studies with differing results have been done on the efficacy of computer-based education. One approach to summarizing the results from many different investigations is to use a *meta-analysis*. To do a meta-analysis one first identifies dozens of studies on the same phenomenon. Then one identifies common variables across all the studies. Finally, one analyses and interprets the results of the different studies on the common variables. For instance, if twenty-five studies showed a significant improvement in student performance when using computers versus when learning in the traditional way and only five studies showed a decrease in performance. The meta-analysis technique is particularly popular in the health sciences where one needs to know whether a particular treatment that has been studied many times but with different results is truly a helpful treatment or not.

Some meta-analyses have shown that computer-assisted instruction is equal or superior to conventional instruction on the following *variables*:

- student achievement, covering both immediate and long-term retention;

- attitude toward the subject matter and the instructor; and

- time to complete the task.

Students taught via computer realize *higher achievement* in significantly less time than the conventionally instructed students (Cartwright, 1993).

However, other meta-analyses have yielded different results. What has been surprising is the dominating influence of the *motivation of the student* and other particulars of the student situation that are quite independent of the content per se. Highly motivated students responded well to material presented on the computer and less highly motivated students responded less well (Chen and Rada, 1996).

The challenge is to be clear about the specifics of the student situation, the learning objectives, and the attributes of the content being used. The *mapping* among students, learning objectives, and content is very complex. For any given students or learning objectives, the tools that will be appropriate may be different.

Hypertext versus Paper

While progress with the use of computers in education has been considerable over the decades, in some occasions paper or other media are more appropriate. *Paper* is a well-known delivery channel. It has the characteristics of familiarity, tangibility, and ease of reading. Essentially everyone can handle paper products. Hypertext is text with links in it that is delivered on a hypertext system, namely a computer (Rada, 1991). It has some capabilities not present in paper, such as the ability to interact with the user but lacks the familiarity, tangibility, and universality.

People have an enormous *competence with paper* documents based on years of practice. A good document flows smoothly, as a theme introduced on one page is carefully continued on the next page. References from one sentence to another are important. For example, in

"Nick hit the ball with his club. It went far."

the 'It' in the second sentence refers to the 'ball' in the first sentence. More subtle and powerful references occur across paragraphs and across sections, and their potency depends on the reader taking a path through the document, which the author has anticipated. With hypertext the path, which a reader is expected to take, is not specified, and thus a given text block must be flexible enough to make good sense when reached from one of many possible directions. Perhaps one cannot write good hypertext, which can also be seen as good text.

A question such as "On what date did Vannevar Bush publish his hypertext paper?" requires the reader to find one fact and may be easily answered with a hypertext system that provides a strong search capability. On the other hand, to answer a question such as "How did the work of Vannevar Bush compare with the work of other hypertext pioneers?" may require browsing several parts of a book. The first type of question is a *search question*, and the second type of question, a *browse question* (Rada and Murphy, 1992).

Users of a hypertext version of the book got the highest-quality answers to search questions, while for browse questions, paper was best. Hypertext systems are useful for searching tasks, and when the links for browsing are tuned to a particular task. In some cases, rather than asking whether hypertext systems will replace paper or not, one should be looking for the ways in which the two media can *complement one another* (Rada, 1991a).

System Standard

While intelligent tutoring systems contain a domain model, a student model, and a pedagogy model more detailed models further facilitate understanding how to build and use such systems. Several international organizations have developed standards for courseware. For instance, the 'Aviation Industry Computer-based-training Committee' (AICC, 2000) produces standards for courseware systems for the aviation industry and certifies the compliance of a product to the standard. The Learning Technologies Standard Committee takes input from other standards organizations, such as the Aviation Committee and produces a standard that is consistent with the other standards (LTSC, 2000). It has developed a model for courseware that is called the Learning Technologies Systems Architecture (see Figure 14 "Learning Systems Architecture").

The flow of information through the Learning Technologies System Architecture follows (Farance and Tonkel, 1998):

- A Learner receives a Multimedia presentation and Learner Behavior is observed.

- An Evaluation process produces Assessment information and sends the Assessment information to a System Coach.

- An Evaluation process creates Performance information that is stored in a Records Database.

- A System Coach requests and receives Performance information from the Records Database.

- A System Coach sends Query Indexes to a Knowledge Library to search for content that is appropriate for the Learner.

- The Knowledge Library stores knowledge, presentations, tutorials, tools, experiments, laboratories, and other learning materials.

- Learning Content is the coded representation of the learning experience, retrieved by the Knowledge Library, and transformed by the Delivery system into an interactive, multimedia learning experience.

This carefully delineated process lends itself to automation.

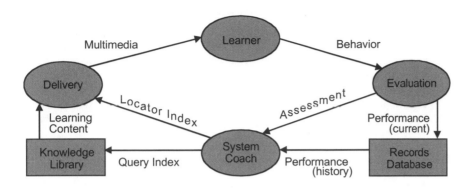

Figure 14: "Learning Systems Architecture". This drawing of the Learning Technologies System Architecture shows the key components and relationships.

The starting point of the Architecture is the delivery of information, via multimedia, to the learner. Feedback, coaching, and learner interaction are necessary to maximize desirable learning experiences and minimize undesirable learning experiences. The behavior of the learner, the evaluation of that behavior, and the assessment that is produced determine where the student "is at". The system coach determines the student's current position from the assessment. Based on the current position, the system coach determines the appropriate action (such as delivery of learning content) to achieve the desired pedagogical objectives. The system coach sends references to lessons, experimentation tools, and suggestions to the delivery system. Feedback loops can recover for errors in human response to the learning experience or can coach, motivate, and direct towards targets and goals.

A single learner does not have a single teacher for his/her lifetime of learning. Performance information is stored in records databases for the purpose of communicating to other teachers so that the next teacher minimizes the amount of observation and evaluation needed to determine the student's background.

A knowledge library may support diverse learning capabilities, strategies, and styles. If a learner is having problems with a particular lesson, an alternate lesson plan may be used to meet the learner's needs. If the lesson is going too fast, then going slower might suffice, but other problems are best solved by adjusting the degree of difficulty. In this case, the knowledge library supports different learning capabilities by having a variety of choices of learning content to meet the varying needs of learners. The learner may interact with the system coach to communicate learning styles. The negotiation may be one-way (learner has sole responsibility for advising, or the system coach has sole responsibility for directing), two-way (learner selects choices from those presented by system coach), or involve other participants, such as parent, employer, mentor, institution, or courseware developer.

The Learning Systems Technology Architecture is a blueprint for a system to support learning. Its delineation of the learning process from the perspective of information flow makes it a basis for designing and implementing software tools for teachers and students. The authors of the Architecture are part of a team developing standards for educational technology. Additional, detailed standards specify how information should be formatted that will be communicated from one component of the system to another component. Software tools that accept information compliant with these standards will support the reuse of system components and potentially encourage the growth of the courseware market.

Producing Interactive Content

The development effort required to produce electronic content is substantial. One company spends about 400 hours in developing each hour of educational material. The inclusion of high quality sound, animation, or video can mean that developing a course from which students gain 1 hour of learning time will require 800 hours. Who can possibly afford such *production costs* and what methods of production are used?

Universities have faculty who are content experts in their disciplines. Are they the appropriate people to develop courseware by themselves (McDonough et al. 1994)? Would a study of what is happening at universities suggest some other approach?

Regional Effort

In the USA, Great Britain, Japan, and elsewhere governments support courseware development. In 1989 the British University Funding Council set up centers to promote the use of computers in education across all United Kingdom higher education institutions (National, 1996). The centers are part of the British effort entitled the *Teaching and Learning Technology Programme* (TLTP). The brief of these *centers* is the promotion of sound technology-based educational practice. Each center focuses on one discipline area, with a senior academic as director of the center and a full-time center manager with content expertise.

The British Computers in Teaching Center for Biology is based at Liverpool University, Great Britain. The Director of that center believes that although high student usage is a crucial factor, it does not necessarily mean that a particular course has to have high student numbers to justify use of computerized content. Content may be reused on other courses, possibly with some customization. Or high usage may refer to consortia developed content, which will be used in similar departments in other institutions. Lecturers in other departments and institutions in Higher Education may be interested in using, customizing and reusing existing content, but they have to know that it exists in the first place. The various Centers have offered some help in this area to their own specific disciplines by *collecting, collating and disseminating information* about content. The important considerations are that content must be easy to obtain, easy to customize and easy to use.

After the spending of tens of millions of dollars and several years' effort, an independent review of the TLTP project was undertaken. Some of the conclusions of that study (Coopers et al. 1996) are summarized next. Institutional support was a criterion for TLTP project selection. Institutions implemented TLTP through five main strategies: staff training, development and support, internal specialist units, awareness raising, strategic coordination, and technological infrastructure development. Such an *institutional focus* is critical to the success of change in higher education. Without a basic level of institutional resourcing, expertise and commitment, the uptake and integration of technologies in support of teaching and learning cannot be guaranteed.

An original TLTP objective was to make teaching and learning more productive and efficient. This objective became less prominent as the program progressed. The emphasis instead switched to *quality improvement*. The academics were more comfortable with the concept of working towards improving quality than improving efficiency.

Although comprehensive dissemination planning was rare, a great deal of effort went into dissemination through surveys, newsletters, road shows, and piloting. Projects did not, however, conduct cost/benefit analyses of such activities. Systematic dissemination plans were not apparent. A developed dissemination plan should have been a pre-condition for funding.

TLTP followed the principle that its content should be *free* to all higher education institutions in Great Britain This approach appears to have dampened the desire of projects to put much effort into dissemination in Great Britain because there would be few resource-related returns to the investment. Project members question whether the product can be maintained without being able to charge for it.

The independent review made two major recommendations for future funding. The first was that emphasis should be placed on implementation and take-up. This requires addressing such areas as cultural change within higher education and the role of teachers in education. The report said "We think funding should be available for this, but *to the market not to the suppliers*". The second area for future funding would be a small amount of new content. To receive such funding a project would have to demonstrate that large student enrollments were possible across institutions, that efficiency would result from using the content, and that no institution alone could support the effort.

Organizational Issues

A delicate balance between *technical and academic* issues must be reached before computers can offer a high-quality, educational experience. As technical environments become more powerful, maintaining this balance becomes more difficult. The organizational issues involved are of paramount importance. As projects move from conceptualization to actual creation, the roles, tasks, and organization change.

There are three *stages in courseware development* (Hopper, 1993):

1. defining what the courseware should do and how it will be used.

2. actually designing and developing the courseware or finding an existing piece of content that could satisfy the requirements decided upon in Stage 1.

3. using the courseware.

Faculty members generally do Stage 1. It appears to be based on the lecturer's own experiences, not on any pedagogical theory, and comes from the desire to improve an existing course or teaching method.

In Stage 2, a common method of courseware production is based on a team development approach. The reasons for the existence of a team and have its constituents vary from project to project. For instance, some projects develop both *course content and software* and others only content. Larger teams are typically involved in developing software than in developing content alone because of the need to have the software speak exactly the language of the computer.

Faculty tends not to know formal models of content development. Most follow an *informal process*. Furthermore, the documentation of the plans tends to be informal. Many university content developers keep plans and processes in their heads. There are few formal planning activities and the main form of communication is verbal. This is possibly due to the informal nature of academia or perhaps to the high degree of flexibility the computer allows.

It is important to maintain any product to stop it falling into disuse and ultimately being unusable. This is an organizational issue. As already stated it is the faculty who conceptualize content and often play a large part in its development. They have tended to see content projects in the same way as they would a publication, i.e. once it is finished and delivered that is the end of the matter. This is highly detrimental to the longevity of the courseware.

The two most important resources for the initial creation of content are human and technical, but its continuation and expansion are mainly dependent on organizational resources. Three different *organizational models* (see Figure 15 "Courseware Organization") have been developed to support courseware development; they are the:

- creator organizational structure,

- integrator organizational structure, and

- orchestrator organizational structure.

The *creator organizational structure* is the traditional academic structure for course design and implementation. An individual faculty member takes on the responsibility for both administration and creation. A person who performs this role is typically called an author or a creator. Where faculty create content, there is an emphasis on the need for technical resources, which would allow a great deal of adaptability and availability. This type of structure does have limitations, as it is dependent on the enthusiasm and talents of an individual who doubtless has other commitments and interests.

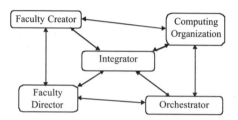

Figure 15: Courseware Organization. The creator, integrator, and orchestrator roles are depicted here.

The *integrator organizational structure* is characterized by the role of the integrator. This refers to an individual who is engaged in a partnership with the faculty. The integrator has responsibility for development but is neither a faculty member nor part of the main computing organization of the university. Projects, which use this model, resembled the traditional lab structure. The universities tend to recognize and support them in similar ways. Consequently this model is limited in the same ways and is found to be financially challenging.

The *orchestrator organizational structure* is characterized by the role of a third organization to support the development of content. This third organization is neither an academic organization nor the main computing organization at the university. Such an organization is most likely to be used when the project is involved in creating its own software tools. It has a distinct set of goals related to the production of content or software. The orchestrator tends to support many content products at one time. This is a particularly dynamic model as it allows the various roles within it to change and grow. Within this model the role of integrator still exits and it is at this point that the academic, technical and orchestration organizations meet. A mutually beneficial relationship is created by using the strengths of the departmentally based projects to provide the content and part of the human resources, while the orchestrator provides support in the form of technical resources and advice.

There is perhaps another organizational model that can be considered which leads from the effect that delivery can have on the content development process. It can be called the *learner construction organizational structure*. The issues of limited time and skills, which are prominent problems in faculty-based development, are often missing from student-based development strategies. Students are greater in number than faculty and may have together more time and skills available. Not only does student-based development have advantages for the project but it also brings benefits to the student. The student gains greater motivation for his or her course as well as improved cognitive skills.

Course Architecture and Life Cycle

Professional content development organizations have formalized methods of working. Consider next a company of 100 full-time courseware specialists that follow well-defined production life cycles (Rada, 1995a).

A course developed by this company has a *standard structure*. Each course is split into modules, which identify one or more subject areas. A module is split into one or more lessons. Each of them will describe one topic. The topic will be provided to the student during a teaching session. A teaching session should be 45 minutes in duration; between two teaching sessions a break has to be allowed.

Recurrent parts are present in each *lesson*, which have the aim to describe contents and give general information about a lesson. These parts are: lesson title, lesson description, and lesson conclusion. The lesson description is a standard format frame, or a series of frames, stating:

- lesson objective,
- what the student will be able to achieve at the end of the lesson,
- pre-requisite background necessary to reach the lesson, and
- lesson length.

The lesson conclusion is a standard format frame, which reports general information when the student has completed the lesson and introduces the next lesson to perform.

The *courseware life cycle* has six phases (see Figure 16 "The Courseware Life-Cycle"). In each phase, there are strictly interconnected intermediate phases. All the phases are subject to quality control in order to establish conformity to the relevant specifications. The quality control is performed on both the result and the methodology used to generate it. Active customer involvement in the process is a must for the project success.

Content product development originates from a *customer request*. The customer request, which is rendered official with the issue of a system document, is the basis for generating a development contract. Starting from the customer request, the project group:

- identifies the goals of the content,
- defines how the goals will be met, and
- plans the activities needed to develop the content.

In the *Requirements and Planning phase* the project group issues the Content Requirement Specification document, which includes hardware and software architecture, applicable teaching strategy, and interconnection between the different components of the courseware. At the same time, the Content Development Plan document is issued containing the planning of activities, the employed resources, and the time schedule. In addition, the Content Test Plan document is produced which describes the testing methodology. At the same time the Quality Assurance group issues the Content Quality Assurance Plan document.

PHASE	DOCUMENTS
Requirements and Planning	Requirements Specification; Development Plan; Quality Assurance Plan
Preliminary Design	Design Specification
Storyboard Production	Storyboard Collection; Storyboard Test Report; Audiovideo Specification
Implementation	Frame Listing; Lesson Test Report
Integration	Trainee Manual; Instruction Manual
Delivery	Configuration List Item Data; Acceptance Test Report

Figure 16: Courseware Life Cycle. The documents, which result from a phase, are listed in the right-hand column of the row describing the phase. The final two phases not listed here are "guarantee" and "maintenance".

The *Review of Requirements* is held to verify the completeness of the requirements and to approve the testing criteria. The following staff takes part in the Requirements Review:

- The Manager,
- The Software Project Quality Representative,
- One or More Customer Representatives,
- The Configuration Management Representative,
- The Systems Technical Manager,
- The Quality Assurance Manager,
- The project Technical Manager, and
- Subject Matter Experts.

At the end of the meeting, a report is issued describing the discussed topics, the problems encountered, the corrective actions to be performed, and the time necessary to complete them.

During the *Design Phase*, the customer is allowed to analyze a sample lesson showing the education strategy and the content graphic, audio, and video. This phase is completed once the Design Review is held. The staff that takes part in the Design Review is basically the same as those who take part in the Requirements Review.

For any single lesson, a *storyboard* will be drafted on paper containing one or more graphic images (drawing or pictures) to describe a particular item inside a section. These images describe what will be implemented on the computer in terms of:

- objects to be drawn on the screen,

- interaction with the trainee,

- text layout,

- audio sentences, and

- flow-charts to describe the logical links among the blocks of frames constituting a particular topic in the section.

The storyboards allow the simulation of the lesson before its implementation on the computer.

The Content Designer, with the possible help of the Subject Matter Expert, issues the storyboards of the current module, on the basis of agreed standards, which are contained in the documents issued during the previous activities. The storyboards, together with the relevant flow-charts, are gathered in the *Storyboard Collection* document.

In the *Implementation phase*, the storyboards are implemented on the computer. All the graphics, texts, and logical links of the lesson are developed. At the same time, the visual and audio material is implemented in a preliminary way. Each module is composed of one or more lessons.

In the *Integration phase*, graphics and text are integrated with the final audio and video. At the same time, the Content Usage Manuals are produced. Those manuals will contain an exhaustive summary of the contents in each lesson in the course. In particular the Manual for the Instructor will contain a list of all tests. A Final System Review is held to analyze and approve the issued documentation, and to examine and approve the content produced. In this phase, the final version of the course is officially delivered to the Customer.

Errors have to be signaled with a document written by the Customer containing:

- complete content identifier,

- description of the frame where the error has occurred,

- error description, and

- description of the conditions in which the error has occurred.

The *error report* will be assessed by the producer to guarantee a quick response. Any modifications to the produced courseware involve an update of the whole documentation and configuration. The corrected content will be submitted to all the tests provided for the integration phase. The customer can request modifications involving substantial variations to the delivered content, but pursuing such modifications will give rise to a dedicated contract.

One of the advantages to a consistent approach to courseware development is that modules become more likely to be interchangeable and reusable. Given the great cost of developing courseware, reuse is attractive. Reusable, instructional templates were identified as contributing to *efficient courseware authoring* over fifteen years ago (Avner, 1979). Theories of how to do courseware reuse are plentiful (Rada, 1995a). The extent to which reuse becomes practical depends on wide-scale adoption of standards.

Summary

For *cognitive learning* one essentially wants to augment the knowledge in a student's mind and thus helps a student behave effectively. Learning strategies can emphasize a spectrum from rote learning to very creative learning. By connecting the learning to real world experiences, the students are positioned and motivated to make extensive changes to their internal model.

One of the most prevalent uses of the computer in supporting interactions that might have otherwise been special to the teacher is the multiple-choice question. From the earliest days of computers with terminals at which users could read text and reply with choices, the multiple-choice question could be placed online. Since the correct answer is pre-determined by the teacher and known to the computer, the computer can mark a student's response. From this simple beginning of multiple-choice questions, enhancements lead to progressively more powerful courseware.

The courseware is more powerful as it incorporates models of the pedagogical process, of the domain, and of students. Then it can take on new interactions with students that guide the student to improved learning as a teacher would do. Many *intelligent tutoring systems* have been developed in research laboratories and some have had practical success, but the spread of them has been limited by a lack of standardization, high start-up costs, and the small marketplace (due, in part, to incompatible, non-standardized systems).

In the end, there will be some kinds of courseware that are appropriate for teaching some subjects to some students and other kinds of content that are appropriate for other subjects and other students. The mapping among the components of this triad is complex and evolving as the characters of the components evolve. Tensions occur when a mapping is imposed that is inappropriate.

The procedures at large authoring enterprises may reflect a manufacturing approach to the development of content. Every step inside the process has a pre-defined before and after step. Every function to be performed is assigned to a specialist role.

Large investments in courseware production with a team approach are not restricted to commercial operations. For instance, the Open University in Great Britain follows a manufacturing approach to content production. The number of likely buyers of the content are identified and when that number merits investing about one million dollars in course production, then a new course is generated with a large team of specialists working to a highly structured, courseware life cycle.

"Classroom". A teacher lecturing to students in a traditional classroom.

Teaching and Class

In this chapter the reader can explore the

- opportunities afforded by teamwork in the classroom,
- back-end and front-end to groupware – software that supports users working together,
- different communication channels that fit into different kinds of group situations,
- details of one case study of an asynchronous classroom,
- impressive efficiency and effectiveness results of a studio course, and
- further potential of peer-peer interactions to support efficiency.

Introduction

Are the teachers and students in the classroom engaged in a formal group activity? By definition each member of a *formal group* should be responsible for one or more distinct activities such that the sum of the activities accomplishes some group objective. Traditional higher education classes are in this sense barely group activities.

In one-to-one computer-based tutoring, the system interacts with one student and attempts to personalize the tutoring to the needs of the student. On the other hand, in a one-to-many collaborative learning environment, the system interacts with a group of students, imparting the subject knowledge using a classroom strategy. In principle an intelligent tutoring system designed for a one-to-one interaction could be augmented for the group or classroom setting. However, current *intelligent tutoring systems* seldom account for group interactions.

Virtual classrooms are means for students to interact with one another or with the teacher (Paloff and Pratt, 1999). Collaborative learning plays a major role in cognitive development.

Piaget (1928) felt that interaction between peers is equally shared. This contrasts with teacher-student interactions, where usually the former is in control and the latter follows what the former professes.

Collaborative writing in the classroom can be beneficial for both students and teachers (Shackelford, 1990). These benefits are based on the principle of feedback and include the rhetorical sense of audience, the psychological power of peer influence, and the transfer-of-learning principle. When students receive feedback on their writing by their peers, it is more likely that they will improve the sense of audience. Feedback can help students sense the progress of the writing. Even students who prefer working alone expressed that their involvement in collaborative activities in their courses was helpful for their work (O'Malley & Scanlon, 1990).

Groupware

Groupware is software that supports and facilitates a group's work (Johnson-Lenz and Johnson-Lenz, 1991). Groupware may support either *synchronous or asynchronous* coordination (Johansen, 1989). Some tasks, such as brainstorming, may benefit from synchronous interaction where all the collaborators are present throughout the task. On the other hand, in some tasks, like group writing, collaborators often work in an asynchronous manner.

In addition to time considerations, groupware can be characterized by the support it provides for the geographical distribution of its users (Rodden, 1991). Group members may work in the same place (e.g. across universities) or in remote places (e.g. software development teams). Groupware can support groups across both time and space boundaries (see Figure 17 "Time and Space"). Groupware may also be characterized by its assumption about the control relations among people. For instance, in a classroom the teacher has strong *control* over the students and the students have little control over one another. Along the *social dimension*:

- mechanistic groupware constrains people to work through explicit forms and procedures; but

- context groupware supports the structuring and browsing of knowledge.

The Coordinator (Winograd and Flores, 1986) system is an example of *mechanistic groupware*. It imposes and constrains group communication to a predefined set of actions and commitments. Communication is mediated through electronic mail. Several message types are defined, and the recipient of each message has to commit to taking an action (Hayes, 1992). Mechanistic groupware suits only certain situations. Mechanistic groupware might be successful in organizations, which already base group work on strict rules and procedures. In more flexible organizational cultures such systems may reduce effectiveness and creativity.

Groupware as context reflects the opposite approach to mechanistic groupware. It is based on the social theory that human systems are self-organizing and encourages open, unrestricted

	Same Time	Different Time
Same Place	Face-to-face	Library
Different Place	Audio video-conference	Email

Figure 17: "Time and space". Dimensions of group work are shown. An example of the type of interaction is indicated in the inner boxes with dimensions labeling the columns and rows.

interaction (Johnson-Lenz and Johnson-Lenz, 1991). Systems in this category do not focus on group dynamics. Their main focus is on user interface tools and tools that allow the structuring and the browsing of social knowledge. This characterization applies to the majority of virtual classroom tools. However, the trend is to more control supported by the virtual classroom and thus a more mechanistic groupware.

Communication

Telecommunication links can provide a useful means of communicating when face-to-face communication is not feasible. Today meetings are often held via audio facilities when they focus on simple tasks, such as information gathering, information exchange, and discussion of ideas. For more complex tasks, such as conflict resolution, people often prefer face-to-face meetings. Is a classroom-learning situation on this scale a relatively simple or complex task?

Video Conferencing

Video was considered early in the twentieth century to be potentially an enormous influence on education. A textbook from that time said (Duggan, 1936):

> Two new kinds of equipment, which have already influenced teaching and are likely to influence it, further are the radio and the motion picture... The motion picture as an aid to teaching began to attract attention early, but the expense, the lack of suitable films and of an efficient manner of using them long prevented their introduction into schools. The matter of expense has become less burdensome by the development in recent years of a standard narrow (16 mm.) film which produces pictures large enough for class use at a greatly reduced cost and which can be shown by means of a portable projector and without fire hazard.

In 1936 people predicted great impacts of new advances in *audio video technology* on the classroom use of audio video tapes, but these predictions were not realized.

The combination of telephone links with television links allows people to hear and see one another at the same time. The first commercial application of the telephone plus television was called the *PicturePhone*. When AT&T introduced the PicturePhone at the 1964 World's Fair the product was expected to sell very well. Julius Molnar, executive vice-president of Bell Laboratories wrote in the Bell Laboratories Record in 1969:

> Rarely does an individual or an organization have an opportunity to create something of broad utility that will enrich the daily lives of everybody. Alexander Graham Bell with his invention of the telephone in 1876, and the various people who subsequently developed it for general use, perceived such an opportunity and exploited it for the great benefit of society. Today there stands before us an opportunity of equal magnitude, PicturePhone service.

Regular users of PicturePhone over the network between Bell Laboratories and AT&T's headquarters agreed that conversations over PicturePhone conveyed important information over and above that carried by voice alone.

The enthusiasm for PicturePhone from its creators at AT&T was not, however, shared by other users. These new users felt self-conscious about being on television and didn't feel that the value gained by the extra information outweighed the equipment or social costs (Egido, 1988). The PicturePhone was a *commercial failure* and highlights the difficulty of predicting how new technology will be accepted by people.

The history of videoconferencing provides a good lesson for developers of educational technology. By the 1970s the enthusiasm misplaced for the PicturePhone had been replaced by a somewhat similar enthusiasm for videoconferencing, which was to allow groups of people to see and hear each other through electronic media and thus avoid large travel costs. *Videoconferencing* has not become as popular as many predicted it would become. The reason for this is partly that people prefer the face-to-face contact that meetings in person support. In two studies of the early 1970s, it was concluded that 85 percent of physical meetings could be replaced with videoconferencing, while a very similar study concluded that only 20 percent of the meetings could be thus substituted. The latter study had taken the extra step of asking people whether they would choose to use videoconferencing as a substitute for a face-to-face meeting.

Research results indicate that video conferencing could be adequate in situations involving giving or receiving information, asking questions, exchanging opinions, solving problems, and generating ideas. In addition the video may allow users to have a sense of presence of other people. The *sense of presence* is an important factor that may affect individual performance within groups. The sense of presence depends on the size of the video screen. The feeling of "presence" is low for normal television screens. A large projection display increases the feeling of presence.

Nevertheless, compared with face-to-face interaction, *video has limitations*, mainly affecting the coordination of interaction (Isaacs and Tang, 1993). Interacting remotely through video makes it difficult for participants to control the floor through body position and eye gaze (it is not possible to ascertain exactly at whom other participants are looking when all the other participants appear on each participant's screen). By the same token users have difficulty pointing at things in each other's space.

To promote interactivity in a class videoconference, *guidelines for teachers* have been designed as follows (Woodruff and Mosby, 1997):

- Include the participants in the conference within the first 5 minutes. Involve them early so they don't turn away. Try a name game, or ask a compelling question that taps their affective domain.

- For group work, select individuals at each site to participate on inter-site teams.

- Using the pre-obtained roster, call on students at both sites by name. Encourage discussion.

- Take as many questions from the distant site as you take from the local site and encourage students at distant sites to answer.

- Devote 30–65 percent of each hour to student activity.

Asking a question can be daunting for students, especially if it means they must get the attention of a remote teacher and talk to a television screen. Teachers can help by noting the body language of remote students and taking the time to query when students seem puzzled or disinterested. Eye contact and use of names both help make students feel more comfortable. These people skills are obvious and natural in a "live" classroom, but may seem awkward in a distance-learning situation. "Eye contact" means looking at the camera and the monitor rather than local students, and teachers might have to make a special effort to attend to remote learners.

Group Hypertext

Hypertext that is shared and updated by multiple users is an opportunity for students and teachers to communicate asynchronously. Early group hypertext systems were in use in the 1960s (Engelbart and English, 1968). Intermedia was a networked hypertext system developed at

Brown University in the mid-1980s (Landow, 1990) and applied to education. "Context32" and "In Memoriam" were two applications of Intermedia for education.

Students in English at Brown used Context32, as part of the Intermedia corpus, to supplement assigned readings. *Context32* was a mixture of materials, study guides, summaries of state-of-the-art scholarship, introductions to basic critical concepts, and original scholarly and critical contributions. Five individuals, who each wrote documents on a set of authors and topics and gathered graphic materials, undertook the development of Context32. Some materials created by others were modified and linked to the original contributions.

Students made contributions to Context32 by:

- creating links among documents present on the system;
- creating text documents (and linking them to others); and
- creating graphics documents (and linking them to others).

Student users created new concept maps in the form of overview or literary relation files, and used earlier ones as templates, making minor modifications and changing the texts.

Tennyson's In Memoriam is a complex, experimental Victorian poem that was an attempt to create new versions of traditional major poetic forms from 133 separate sections. Each section is a poem that can stand on its own. It is particularly appropriate for hypertext representation as it makes extensive use of echoing, allusion, and repetition. The entire poem was placed in Intermedia and linked to:

- variant readings from manuscripts,
- published critical commentary; and
- passages from works by other authors.

In 1988, members of a graduate seminar added more than a hundred documents, each commenting specifically on one or more sections of the poem and on one another's work. The first assignment for the project required them to create five documents to append to individual sections of the poem. Each week members of the seminar read the contributions of others, added more documents and then made links. The final assignment of the project involved students putting online the texts of poems by another poet that had obvious relevance to individual sections of Tennyson's work. The "In Memoriam" project was successful in promoting collaboration among students for the sake of learning. However, it took the Web a few years later to provide a platform on which large numbers of users could engage in collaborative learning through group hypertext.

Bulletin Boards

A *bulletin board* is a kind of structured, archived, asynchronous, discussion or can also be seen as group hypertext. One such system was developed at San Francisco State University (Klavins, 2000) and is organized into three main levels. The first level is the class. Each class is organized into topics (the second level) where the coursework is contained. The third level contains conversations between students and instructors in response to the material presented in each topic (see Figure 18 "Bulletin Board").

The *Geography course* at Boston University (Annis, 1992) extensively used computer conferencing. The management of the course, assignment-giving, and considerable interaction between instructor and students was conducted through a semester-long computer conference. Students corresponded on topics in the computer conference. Students added comments, raised questions and carried on student-to-student debate, and wrote short critiques of assigned readings and of each other's work. As students became more skillful network users, they would reinforce the computer conferences by importing relevant material from other conferences on the electronic highways. Often, vast amounts of highly up-to-date, technical material could be found that would carry the discussion far beyond the initial class presentation.

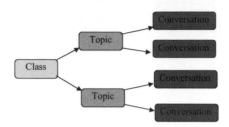

Figure 18: Bulletin Board. This system has a hierarchical structure of a class that includes topics and conversations.

A special facility was created by a graduate student who applied her background in tropical ecology and computer programming to construct the shell and initial biological population for a *virtual rainforest*. This is a text-based simulation of a rainforest environment, something like the popular adventure games on personal computers. In this case, a "player" receives messages something like, "You hear a fluttering screech and look up through the green canopy where you see a troupe of howler monkeys..." Though kinetically less dramatic to students than the competition in video arcades, such "games" are intriguing for several reasons. They can be freely accessed through the Internet from virtually any networked campus computer, and they can accommodate hundreds of players in real time who are working interactively within the created environment. Their educational content can be developed in highly sophisticated ways by succeeding generations of players and rainforest-makers. For example, the plant and animal population of the "virtual rainforest" could be biologically expanded; slash-and-burn farmers, cattle ranchers, and ecotourism operators; and so on could populate the forest.

The aforementioned "virtual rainforest" facility extends the notion of computer conferencing into what some call MOOs. *MOO* software is a derivative of a multi-user dungeon. The multi-user dungeon game software allows people to play across the Internet in real time or synchronously. By adding programs to the MOO program one can extend the text chat facilities so that various messages or actions get invoked on the basis of a single command introduced by a participant. Entire virtual classes can be based on MOOs (Diversity, 2000).

Multiple Channel

Multiple modalities (Rada, 1995b) can be combined in one virtual classroom. What benefit would putting all the tools into one classroom have? One experiment to address this question is described next.

Three groups of students at geographically distinct locations were asked to solve an engineering design problem using a multimodal, groupware system (Gay and Lentini, 1995). Students were given two hours to design a windmill, which would produce two volts under the forced air from a hair dryer. The groups were given tasks analogous to those of a main contractor and two subcontractors, but the specific tasks of each group were left ambiguous to force the students to negotiate the boundaries of their tasks.

The groupware system consisted of *multiple communication technologies* and multimedia databases. The communication resources were all three-way, and each channel was active throughout the session. The resources were as follows:

- a three-way, closed circuit video-conferencing system which allowed all groups to see and hear all of the activities in the other groups,

- a terminal conferencing system which allowed students to type messages on their computer and send them to their collaborators, and

- another part of the terminal conferencing system, which allowed the students to draw a design on one screen and have it appear on the other two.

The multimedia databases included:

- an interactive multimedia database of engineering information which contained information on each of the subject areas the students would need to address in their design: gears, structures, aerodynamics, power, and generators, and

- scanned engineering textbooks, which also covered the subject areas that would need to be addressed by the students.

There was a link between *student activity and technological resource* used, and this was a critical part of how the students used the system. The students, to either increase the depth of the discussion or increase the breadth of the discussion, used the multiple channels. Using multiple channels to increase depth involved using more than one channel to converse about one topic, while using multiple channels to increase breadth involved conversation on multiple topics, with each topic on one channel.

The ability to use multiple representations allowed the students to supplement a mental and video representation of the design artifact with a drawing that showed details not immediately obvious from looking at the assembled design. Increasing the depth of the interactions allowed students to more effectively communicate their meanings and create much richer representations of the designs. The use of multiple channels to increase breadth proved especially useful when one group member was engaged in a time-consuming activity on one channel. Using the breadth available via multiple channels also became important near the end of the session when the groups had to transmit a great deal of information in very little time. The *mapping* between the technology that is appropriate and the student-learning objective is a complex mapping. No one technology is right for all learning objectives.

Virtual Classroom

The application of information technology to support a group of students working together under the guidance or direction of a teacher may be called a 'virtual classroom' application. This term 'virtual' means something different in the information technology discipline than it means elsewhere. Elsewhere 'virtual' tends to mean 'false' whereas in the information technology subculture, the term 'virtual' means 'transcend'. Thus 'virtual memory' transcends the limits of physical memory. The term 'virtual classroom' means a classroom that transcends the limits of the physical classroom by exploiting information technology.

Roxanne Hiltz and Murray Turroff at the New Jersey Institute of Technology (NJIT) were some of the first people to develop a 'virtual classroom' software system, and they have trademarked the term. The NJIT *Virtual Classroom*™ was specifically designed to support collaborative learning, including discussions, student presentations, joint projects, debates, and role-playing games (Turroff, 1995). Participation is generally asynchronous. An *asynchronous classroom* is one in which the students and teacher interact without needing to be synchronized. Thus the teacher might put an assignment on the Web one day, a student read it anytime later, and answer it yet later. Typically there is a broad time schedule in that the course starts at some date and over some weeks students must submit certain exercises and take certain tests. A correspondence course handled by paper mail could be an example of an asynchronous classroom, but students in such a course might not have any interaction with other students.

System

The Virtual Classroom environment can be used in, at least, two ways:

- Face-to-face plus Virtual Classroom: This can vary from adding system use to enrich on-campus courses conducted by traditional means to distance courses where system use is supplemented by one or two face-to-face meetings.

- No face-to-face but Virtual Classroom: This may be augmented with the use of print media in the form of textbooks or course notes, videos, or CD-ROM.

The Virtual Classroom in each of these modes requires different management than a traditional course requires. Most videos are filmed by NJIT in its classroom and then distributed to remote students on videotape. The Virtual Classroom is used for assignments and additional discussions.

The principal feature of the NJIT Virtual Classroom is called the *conference*. The conference is a stored transcript of a discussion. It has a membership list and a comment-reply structure. There is a full indexing capability for each conference that is especially useful since a typical class discussion may exceed one thousand comments. The conference automatically tracks for each user what is new and what activities or assignments the user has or has not seen or done. In one mode, if the instructor asks a discussion question, then every student must supply an answer before he or she can see the answers of the other students. This feature encourages each student to do independent thinking about the issue.

Student Experiences

The NJIT Virtual Classroom has been used in teaching many courses. One of the salient conclusions is that students must be *actively guided*. It does not 'work' to simply make the Virtual Classroom available and tell students that they can use it to ask questions about the readings or discuss aspects of the course at any time. If it is not a 'required' and graded, integral part of the course, the majority of the students will never use it at all; and those who start to use it, will generally decide that 'nothing is going on there' and will stop using it (Hiltz, 1995).

If students who take most of their courses on campus are permitted to, they may choose to take a significant portion of their courses via a "distance" mode such as Virtual Classroom. This is because they experience scheduling conflicts with other courses, their jobs, or their family obligations, which mean that they either must take a 'distance' course, or take longer to complete their degrees. In the fall of 1995, for instance, about half of the students enrolled in the Virtual Classroom plus Video undergraduate courses took the majority of their degree courses on campus, and half were distance students who took the majority of their courses in distance modes.

Numerous studies have been done of the reaction of students to the Virtual Classroom. On post-course questionnaire, students were asked a series of questions about their course, the instructor, and their experiences. One can conclude that

- mastery of course material in the Virtual Classroom is equal or superior to that in the traditional classroom, and

- Virtual Classroom students report higher subjective satisfaction with the Virtual Classroom than the traditional classroom on some dimensions and not on others.

Most of the answers to questions showed *no significant differences* among modes. The differences in course and instructor ratings are more affected by factors other than whether the class is online or not.

Virtual Classroom students report that they are more likely to *stop attending class* when they are busy with other things. Since the class does not meet at any particular time, it is easy to postpone it, and this procrastination all too easily turns into falling seriously behind.

Figure 19: "Traditional Classroom". Long lines of chairs with built-in writing surface all facing the blackboard. Otherwise the classroom manifests no other use of technology – just desks and a blackboard.

Teacher Costs

What are the *costs of teaching* with the NJIT Virtual Classroom? Teaching with the Virtual Classroom and videotapes can be more demanding than traditional face-to-face lectures. The first time one prepares the materials for weekly Virtual Classroom modules and moderates the conferences, this is much more work than just delivering lectures face-to-face.

Once the course has had its basic delivery materials and videotapes developed:

- If the class has less than 25 students, the actual amount of work to conduct it is about the same as for a traditional class.

- The amount of work is directly proportional to the number of students, since there is no limit to the amount of time each student can ask questions.

- For more than about 30 students, class conferences have to be divided to be manageable, thus increasing the faculty workload substantially.

Institutions may initially think that virtual classes are a "cheap" way to deliver education. However, if full-time faculty conducts the courses, more of their time is required. There is much to be done in discovering which tasks can be offloaded from faculty to lower-priced teaching assistants, without substantially decreasing the quality of the product delivered.

The traditional lecture is very efficient in terms of teaching time. The teacher stands before an arbitrarily large group of students and delivers a lecture delivered perhaps similarly in the previous version of the same course (see Figure 19 "Traditional Classroom"). The students sit quietly and listen though they have a sense of being properly educated, as this mode of delivery is what they have come to expect of higher education. An online classroom that simply delivers a lecture on the computer screen seems less intimate and interactive than the physical classroom. However, with either the physical or online versions of the classroom the teacher can manage much more interaction for students than is traditionally done.

Other Cases

While virtual classrooms are being used more and more frequently, confusion still reigns as to when such teaching is or is not appropriate. In 1996 students in a Social Statistics course at California State University, Northridge were randomly divided into two groups, one taught in a traditional classroom and the other taught virtually on the World Wide Web. Text, lectures, and exams were standardized between the conditions. Quantitative results demonstrated the virtual class scored an average of 20 percent higher than the traditional class on both examinations (Schutte, 1997).

Post-test results indicate the virtual class had significantly higher perceived peer contact, and time spent on class work, than did the traditional class. Much of the performance difference is attributed to student collaboration rather than the technology itself. In fact, the highest performing students in both classes reported the most *peer interaction*. Students in the technology group were required to communicate with one another and the teacher extensively. Students in the traditional classroom situation had no such explicit requirement. This kind of confounding variable is common in virtual classroom experiments and makes rigorous comparison of one method of teaching to another difficult. Faculty must pay attention to the issue of collaboration, whether in the traditional classroom or in the virtual classroom.

Another study concerns a graduate chemistry course taught as an email discussion from the University of Nebraska to high school chemistry teachers (Liu, 1996). Twenty-one students started in the graduate chemistry course, but only nine students completed the course. The study concluded that the

- causes of incompletion are technological problems and pedagogical immaturity; and

- though relatively easy and inexpensive, communication entirely via email is inadequate to satisfy the communication needs of individuals involved in distance-learning courses.

The high school chemistry teachers were involved in a day-to-day world of meeting face-to-face with their own students. To engage in a course where they were the students and for which all interaction was by email did not fit into their workflow or way of life.

Studio Course

In some disciplines, particularly the science and engineering disciplines, a course will often require students to meet in different types of rooms for different types of work at different times. The lecture may include hundreds of students at one time. A laboratory session may occur once each week, and students work under loose supervision in this laboratory to explore hands-on some aspect of the course. A recitation session may additionally be held each week in which students meet as a small group with a teaching assistant to discuss problems with the reading material or textbook assignments. A *studio course* combines these three course activities, and students meet always in the same room at the same time and face in the one meeting a combination of lecture, recitation, and lab. With the addition of computer-supported learning the studio course method has been shown to have very impressive educational results, as demonstrated in the Physics Studio Courses at Rensselaer Polytechnic Institute.

Figure 20: "Studio". Students with computers in one room where they can work together or alone and are monitored by the teacher.

Studio Course Structure

The *Physics Studio Course* at Rensselaer includes:

- a method of meeting with students face-to-face and
- a courseware infrastructure.

The structure of the studio course is unrelated to the lecture-based courses that preceded it. There are four contact hours instead of the six used by the lecture course (RPI, 2000).

A single facility (see Figure 20 "Studio") serves all of the contact hours, instead of having separate facilities for *lecture, recitation, and laboratory.* In the facility a graduate student assists the mentor. This permits a different personal and cultural approach to small group attention and feedback. The assisting presence provides a 'safety net' for instructor-student interactions, filling in if the mentor is unavailable or unable.

The role of the student in the classroom is one of *localized control.* The students are responsible for each activity to which they are assigned and perform several activities each class. The exact style in which this is accomplished is flexible to each student, allowing for differences in learning style, interest, and preparation. Because they have local control of the tools, a student may explore opportunities to approach the subject matter from different directions, should the need occur. Students are encouraged to work together to solve a problem or achieve understanding.

The role of the instructor in the Studio Course is different from that in a lecture. The instructor is actually a *mentor* that guides the students through a series of self-controlled discoveries. The students are required to exploit their role as experimenters. The mentor focuses on guiding the progress of the class, correcting pitfalls, and expanding on questions that rise from the material.

The Physics Studio course uses courseware. A key reason for this is the computer's ability to help students understand various *representations of physical phenomena.* The leap from representation to representation is daunting to most students yet critical to the conceptual understanding of the phenomenon. The Physics Studio Course uses courseware that allows the student to view the many different physics representations at the same time.

Results

Experience with the studio course shows that students were able to *complete the material faster and learn it better* than the same group taught in the traditional way in the previous year by the same instructor. These results have been repeatedly confirmed at Rensselaer Polytechnic Institute with the studio courses. Students also prefer these classes to the traditional courses.

Additionally, the Studio Courses have been shown to *cost the university less* to teach. The arguments behind this reduction in costs follow. The cost of the traditional class in terms of hours of faculty and staff time is compared to the Studio Course as follows:

- The traditional method requires 6 sections of 48 students each. Each section meets 3 times a week for 1 hour over 10 weeks. This 30-hour per term per section time gives 180 lecture hours. Six student assistants are also utilized, each at 12 hours per week.

- For the studio course the standard format of 30 one-hour lectures per term is replaced by 10 two-hour studio sessions, where 48 students meet with the mentor in a workstation-equipped classroom. Students are expected to learn independently to a substantial degree, using the studio, other computer labs, or their own machines. Student assistants work as previously.

The high-cost labor of the faculty has been reduced from 30 hours/term/section to 20 hours/term/section. This major reduction has to be weighed against the technology costs (Massy and Zemsky, 1995). However the technology costs can be amortized, whereas the faculty costs are fixed and recurrent. One expects that the technology costs will be less than the faculty costs in the long run, if not in the beginning. There is much interest in the results of the Studio Course method of teaching. Certainly a teaching method that simultaneously *reduces costs and improves learning* is worthy of support.

Efficiency and Peer-Peer Assessment

The studio course achieves efficiency through reduced lecturing and employs a variety of means to enhance learning to include use of courseware and encouragement of peer-peer interactions. How does the teacher assure that peer-peer interactions are proceeding well without needing to monitor each and every peer-peer interaction? Peer-peer classrooms help students interact with one another in exercise answers and comments in constrained ways. Can such a classroom improve efficiency and effectiveness? *Efficiency* relates to the ratio of student-student/student-teacher interactions. *Effectiveness* is defined as perceived quality. The classroom system is asynchronous and focuses on students having assignments, doing exercises online, and giving feedback to one another.

1996 and 1997 Version

A course titled the "Design and Analysis of Algorithms" was taught in the fall of 1996. A standard paper textbook was used with the course. The flowchart for the system shows students submitting exercise answers and comments on those answers or other comments (see Figure 21 "Flowchart of System"). Students can request the computer to calculate the current grade of students at any time. This grade is computed according to several parameters. For every day after the due date a submission loses 10 percent of its value. The average score assigned to the submission by other students is also directly proportional to the value of the submission. The students graded one another's work with the help of the computer that monitored the time of submissions and tallied all results.

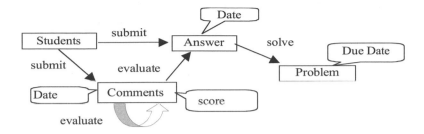

Figure 21: Flowchart of System. This diagram shows the students submission of answer and comments each date stamped.

The teacher guided the work by having created the mechanism of the course and by monitoring for fair and productive performance by all. The ratio of comment submissions to exercise submissions was 0.3. This is relatively *inefficient* in terms of how few comments were made.

The students were asked to complete a *course evaluation* form. The school average score was 4.1 but the average in this class was only 3.3. Students were not satisfied with the course and, among other things, wanted to see further evidence of the expertise of the teacher and made comments like "lectures would be better".

Another course refining the methods of the fall 1996 course was offered in spring 1997. The grading program now took note of whether students had completed a predefined minimal amount of work per topic. This extended the *mechanistic assessment* part of the system.

About 1,000 exercise submissions were made and about 2,000 comments. The ratio of comments to exercise submissions was 2.0, which is highly efficient. Class evaluations were done on a monthly basis and showed an average effectiveness rating of 4.9 on a scale of 1 to 5 were 5 was best and the average in the school was about 4.0. Thus this course was both *efficient and effective.* The increased controls in the groupware had a beneficial effect.

1998 Version

The Classroom system was modified and used in two classes in spring 1998. Each student was required to log onto the system regularly with a unique identifier and password. The system characteristics are seen through the main windows that are available to the student called "Assign", "Edit/View", "Grades", and "Communications".

On going to the 'Assign' window the student can see exactly each exercise assignment and comment assignment confronting the student for the next deadline (see Figure 22 "Assignments"). When providing a comment, the student must also provide a score along three dimensions of clarity, completeness, and correctness. Each exercise answer and comment must have some minimum number of characters, otherwise the computer warns the student of the shortness and refuses to accept the submission till it is lengthened. Students used a paper textbook as a complement to the online system. In that paper book the student's exercises were described, and the computer pointed students to the exercises in the paper book.

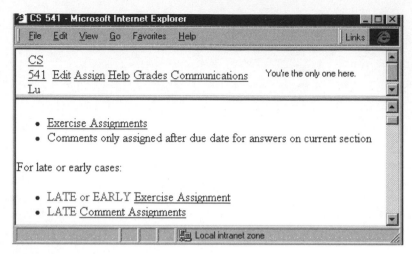

Figure 22: "Assignments". This screen of the Peer-Peer Classroom shows in the upper frame the links to different lower frames.

The computer keeps track of all work performed and students get credit for all submissions that they make to the system. The number of points earned for an exercise answer submission depends on the comment scores assigned to the answer. The system also monitors the comments. Each comment initially earns the commenting student a fixed, default credit. Subsequently this credit is weighted by a factor that depends on the pattern of commenting scores. The standard deviation of all comment scores assigned by any particular student is computed, and more than some pre-specified amount penalizes the student for not varying comment scores. From the "Grade" window the student sees the cumulative points earned so far and the breakdown by category (see Figure 23 "Grades"). A final letter grade is automatically computed based on the typical distribution of letter grades in other courses in the school (for instance, if the top x students get an A, then the top x students in this virtual classroom also get an A).

Students are assigned to do three times as many comments as exercise answers. Every answer is expected to get three comments by some systematic rotation of student commenter so that one student does not repeatedly get assessed by the same other student. The computer checks the range of scores assigned to a particular answer by the three commenting students. If the range of comment scores exceeds some threshold, then the students are issued a warning. If the students do not modify their grades to be more in accord with one another, then each of the commenting students loses some credit.

The two weightings of a student's comment scores are based on the two assumptions:

- variance in grading within a student's responses is desirable and
- variance in grading between students' responses is not desirable.

In other words, students must exercise discrimination in their across-student grading. However, several students commenting on one other student should not show gross disparity in their assessments. The teacher can grade any exercise answer or student comment. The teacher's scores can have a significant impact on a student's earned grades.

One of the two courses taught with the previous system was a required, undergraduate course entitled "Computers and Society". Forty-three students finished the course. The exercises came from the course textbook entitled *Social Issues in Computing* (Huff and Finholt, 1994).

Students did all their assigned work. A survey determined that the students had a wide range of backgrounds, found the course convenient, but did not feel that they learned much. Fifty-five percent of the students disagreed with the statement: "I find that the comments given by other students are fair and accurate."

Also in the spring of 1998 a graduate course was taught using the same system used to teach the undergraduate course. The graduate course was an elective entitled "Artificial Intelligence" and used the textbook by Russell and Norvig (1995). Ten students finished the course.

Again the students completed all assigned work. Both the length of answers and the length of comments increased significantly between the first and second half of the graduate course, whereas the opposite was true of the undergraduate course.

The same survey that was submitted to the undergraduate course was also submitted to the graduate course. For the question "I feel that I have learned the material presented in the class" 75 percent of the students either agreed or strongly agreed, whereas basically the opposite was true for the undergraduate course. These students felt that they had learned effectively and that the course was well managed. For reasons that include

- the greater appropriateness of the textbook questions to an answer-comment format,
- the smaller class size that permitted more intimacy, and
- the elective nature of the course and thus the voluntary participation of the students,

The students in the graduate course felt much better about the course than the students in the undergraduate course.

The instructor achieved the correct level of difficulty with the graduate course but not with the undergraduate course.

In the graduate course the length of comments significantly increased in the latter part of the course, whereas for the undergraduate course the opposite happened. These are direct measures of work effort and tendency and indirect indicators of attitude.

The teacher should have been monitoring these phenomena more closely and taking corrective action for the ineffective undergraduate course. Such monitoring is easy to do since all transactions are stored in the database and accessible with various tools that can present summary information.

System features to support teacher commenting on comments were not completed till late in the course. The teacher now can intervene at any time and comment on answers or on other comments, and thus by making more comments a teacher can attempt to compensate for deficient student expertise.

Students need to be taught that comments should explore the subject matter by showing where the answer that is being assessed matches the conceptual model of the commenter and where it does not match.

For this the questions themselves have to be challenging but also someone or some mechanism needs to exist to assure that student responses are of high quality and indicate learning is occurring (Warren and Rada, 1998).

In a collaborative learning environment, where the goal is split into subtasks to be performed by peers, peers may be assigned *roles*. In general, the two most obvious roles are those of executor and reflector, where executor solves the problem and reflector observes and comments on the problem solving (Blaye et al. 1991).

For a peer, the system should maintain a model of these two roles and support them differently. In addition to this breakdown by task-specific roles further breakdowns might occur along other criteria.

Figure 23: "Grades". This screen shows the grades of a particular student. Displayed is the scoring decomposed into various categories At the bottom, the student's total score and relative ranking along with a letter grade are shown.

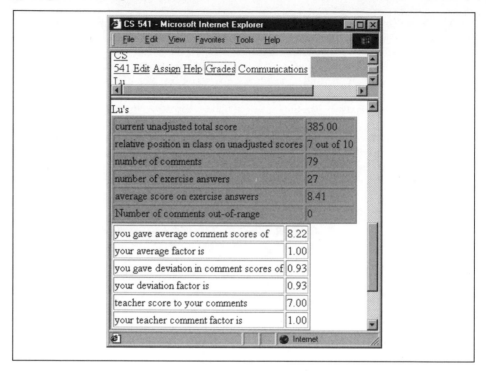

Meta-analysis

Studies of the effectiveness of distance education courses have been ongoing for many years. In 1928, R. E. Crump published "Correspondence and Class Extension Work in Oklahoma". In the work of the 20s and 30s the emphasis was on correspondence courses and moved later into television and radio. Of course, contemporary emphasis tends to be on Internet supported courses (Bonk and King, 1998). In one listing of hundreds of studies done since the 1920s, the fundamental conclusion is that no fundamental differences in quality between face-to-face class and virtual class have been demonstrated (Russell, 1997).

Collaborative learning systems can be classified along dimensions of control, tasks, domains, and roles (Kumar, 1996). The *control* of collaborative interactions refers to the mode of delivery of the collaborative environment by the system. A collaborative learning system can take an active part in analyzing and controlling collaboration or act just as a delivery vehicle for collaboration. Depending on the amount of control embedded within a system, collaborative learning systems can be classified anywhere in the range between active and passive.

In a given collaborative learning environment the collaborating peers could be faced with different types of *task* to perform. The tasks could be enumerated independently of the subject domain that has been taught. For individual learning a popular taxonomy of tasks looks at eight different learning tasks from simple fact acquisition to sophisticated generation of new information.

In general, collaborative learning is found effective in *domains* where peers engage in skill acquisition, joint planning, categorization, and memory tasks. In collaborative learning domains, the domain knowledge to be imparted is complex, hierarchical, and requires deep understanding of each level in the hierarchy. It is difficult to observe a conceptual change if the task is purely procedural and does not involve much understanding. Some domains are less shareable than others, like solving anagrams since the processes involved are not easy to verbalize. Domains like air-traffic control are inherently distributable and hence can be effectively learned with the support of collaborative learning systems (Dillenbourg et al. 1996).

An examination of 226 studies comparing cooperative learning with individual learning showed net advantages to cooperative learning. While much remains unknown about the relationship between interaction and learning in class, many researchers agree that *cooperation and achievement* are positively related (Edelson et al. 1995; Novick and Fickas, 1995).

The bottom line is that the mapping among

- students and teachers,
- their tools and methods, and
- the learning objectives and content

is a *complex mapping*. There is not one specific tool that will be helpful for all students and all learning objectives, but rather the appropriate mapping must be carefully considered on a case-by-case basis. This complex mapping applies to all applications of information technology (Rice and Shook, 1990).

Conclusion

The relationship between technology and the education environment is a reciprocal one. Therefore, a new technology does not exert a singular force on the people who adopt it, nor is its meaning shared equally by all. *Pre-existing social patterns* alter responses to the use of such technologies. New computer tools are affecting the ways in which teaching is accomplished, and in turn, existing patterns of education are shaping the evolution of these highly malleable tools.

The *richest communication* occurs when people are physically face-to-face, and the most sophisticated technology for connecting people with audio and video has not been able to substitute for face-to-face communication. One must understand the principles of education, groups, and of technology to properly develop or apply educational groupware.

One might wonder why earlier technologies, such as the *phone*, have not been used more extensively in the classroom. Limited evidence suggests such a tool can enhance learning in the classroom. However, the phone evidently does not fit the culture of the classroom.

Groupware can support synchronous and asynchronous communication across arbitrary geographic distances. The communication tools can handle text, audio, and video. However, even with the most expensive equipment the value to people of a virtual meeting may not match the value of a face-to-face meeting.

The conclusions about *cost-effectiveness* of groupware are not straightforward. For instance, the creators of the New Jersey Institute of Technology Virtual Classroom claim that it costs more to teach that way than otherwise, but that it is better for students. The Rensselaer Polytechnic Institute Physics Studio people claim that the physics studio reduces costs and improves the quality of education. Certain studio courses have found a niche in which decent courseware exists for a topic and in which small gains can be made by combining limited groupware with conventional means of student teacher and student-student interaction.

Numerous virtual classroom environments have been developed. Since the popularity of the Web, each virtual classroom on the Web can become immediately accessible to a large number of people. The challenge now is partly to standardize. This means in part making clear the design of the systems but more importantly coming to agreement about what this design should be and how components will communicate. Such *standardization* has not occurred but should.

The typical analysis made by academics of cost focuses on the costs to the educational organization as represented by the teachers. It does not pay attention to the *costs to the students*. For some students getting an education by going to where the teacher is physically located may preclude that student getting the education. The costs are not reasonably measured only in terms of the costs to the teacher to teach the students currently being taught.

The impact of the virtual classroom relates to the impact of the classroom on the *students' social behavior*. One anecdote in this regard follows (Black, 1997):

> By day, Michael Blezien is a maintenance manager at Santafill/U.S.A. Waste Services, where he oversees a fleet of about 100 garbage trucks that serve southeastern Wisconsin, just as he has for the last 15 years. By night, Bleizen presides over the "Keepers of the Page," a group of 15 HTML authors dedicated to "the betterment and advancement of HTML and Web page skills." After meeting in an introductory Web course at ZDNet University, the self-described "tribe" decided to continue they're learning among themselves through online interaction, continuing education, and live conferencing.

> "There were four or five of us who got fairly tight," said Bleizen, who is looking for a change after 26 years in the sanitation business. "So after the class, we formed a Web group for people that wanted to stay abreast of Web design issues, people who were really serious about pursuing a career."

To what extent is the virtual classroom an extension of the traditional lecture hall in which students are presented material and later take exams? Are there circumstances under which the virtual classroom allows a new kind of culture to develop in the classroom, which is not possible in the traditional classroom?

The Peer-Peer Classroom has been designed to automate the workflow that is associated with extensive use of peer-peer assessment. Under certain conditions it can have a profound impact on efficiency and effectiveness. The key to success includes the right level of difficulty of assignments and adequate quality control from the teacher.

As the teacher shifts from being the sage on the stage to being the guide on the side, the importance of roles for students and others becomes increasingly apparent. Furthermore, the information technology support for education, particularly via the Web, facilitates the computerized support for student-student and student teacher interactions in ways that can be finely defined and tracked (Rada et al. 1989). Essentially one wonders whether the technologies of groupware and artificial intelligence might become an aspect of the *intelligent virtual classroom*.

Figure 24: "University". The campus of a state university where thousands of students come to live and study is a complex organization.

Administering Universities

In this chapter the reader learns about

- the history of universities and information technology,
- trends in delivering degrees online,
- models of higher education in terms of accounting and management,
- a generic method of quality control based on an international standard for quality processes,
- features of existing university information systems, and
- a common architecture for a university information system.

Introduction

Given that teaching and learning occur, one of the next concerns is the *administering* of the university. How shall this administration be done? Under what conditions can the computer do some of the administering? The fears of academics are particularly reflected in the title of a popular book on the subject entitled *Dancing With the Devil, Information Technology and the New Competition in Higher Education* (Katz, 1999).

Models of organizations are critical to successful automation. What models of universities exist? If one looks at the flow of resources, can one associate that flow with the flow of information in a way that leads to better management?

> The disadvantage of men not knowing
> the past is that they do not know the
> present. History is a hill or high point
> of vantage, from which alone men see
> the town in which they live or the age
> in which they are living. (Chesterton,
> 1933)

Figure 25: "The Value of History".

Quality control is one critical aspect of management. In some senses, one might say that all management is ultimately about achieving quality. What is known about quality control in universities that could be systematically applied in the information systems that are used to help run universities?

Given that administrators do not want to reinvent the wheel, they must understand what exists in the marketplace of *available tools* to facilitate their work. What systems do universities use? What functions do these systems provide and how much effort must administrators invest in tailoring the functionality to their specific situation?

Is there standard *information architecture* for a university that guides the construction of software to support the administration of universities? With standard information architecture for universities could exchange information without the barriers of incompatible information structures and functions.

History of Universities and Technology

At the social level, education aims to perpetuate culture. What have institutions, such as state or church, done over the centuries to extend methods of teaching? Understanding the past is key to understanding the present (see Figure 25 "The Value of History").

Millennia Past

About *five thousand years ago* the Egyptians developed the first *formal systems of schooling*. The vast majority of the population was not privy to this formal education as it was restricted to the privileged classes and ultimately controlled by the priesthood (Mulhern, 1959). The Egyptian civilization was advanced for its time and included extensive agricultural irrigation, building of massive architectural monuments to the aristocracy by armies of slaves, and enshrinement of education paths for the select few. A cultural and vocational educational system was maintained that helped perpetuate the civilization.

Throughout the educational process the few Egyptians who were students learned by *imitation of traditional forms*. The child spent the first few years at home and then was at university during the days. The memorization of texts was emphasized. Discipline in universities was severe and could include flogging and solitary confinement in prison for months for mere neglect of duty.

The Chinese educational system has a history remarkably different from that of the Western World. Two thousand years ago the Chinese had already standardized their educational system. Students were tested on fixed curricula at certain ages in every village and could slowly pass from one level of education to another, as they were able to reproduce from memory certain documents. The most successful students were tested in the nation's capital under precise conditions that included locking each student in a fixed-size brick cell for several days. "By requiring set standards and prescribing teaching methods and uniform syllabuses, and by establishing controlling bodies of literary superintendents, the examination system assumed a systematic comprehensiveness unknown in the West before the mass education systems of the early nineteenth century" (Cleverley, 1991). Textbooks, tools for writing, classrooms, and exams were all highly institutionalized by the state.

Medieval Times

One thousand years ago in the Western World formal education was dominated by the church and for the purposes of the church. Bishops and abbots exercised educational control under authority delegated to them by the pope. Support of monastic, cathedral, song, and parish universities came, in part, from church revenues and, in part, from fees paid by students, and from gifts of their relatives and friends to teachers and universities. Despite a seeming variety of universities, the masses were illiterate. There was no compulsory education. The ecclesiastical and feudal nobility viewed the servile condition of laborers as a reflection of God's will. Although lay teachers were allowed, the preacher was the primary teacher, and *religious education* was the main goal.

It was the enrichment of the program of some cathedral universities that led to universities. The *first university* was the University of Bologna in Bologna, Italy in the *twelfth century A.D.* This and other universities while affiliated in some way with the church tended to have relative liberty to do as they saw fit in the teaching of non-religious topics.

The universities grew up to prepare men for the professions of law, medicine, theology, and teaching. Some study in the arts faculty was typically a prerequisite to study in the other faculties. The *authority of Aristotle* was viewed as final on all subjects on whom he had written. All teachers used the method of lecture with syllogistic argumentation settling issues even in medicine and law. Books were few, and students relied much upon class notes, which they often *memorized*.

The first universities had no building of their own, or equipment, and their teachers lectured wherever they found a room or a vacant lot. Paris gave its faculty of arts a small street for university purposes. Student fees paid directly to the professor supported the first professors. This was a kind of *medieval virtual university* in that it transcended fixed physical structures

When students have produced their masterpieces, they were inducted into the gild of master scholars. The degree of the master craftsman in learning came to be called the Master's or Doctor's degree, the latter coming to be used for graduates of the 'superior' faculties. The title of Bachelor arose of the practice of permitting students, after four or five years of study, to lecture on the *Organanon* of Aristotle for a few years prior to their graduation. Such a lecturer was called a *Bachelor*, a title long borne by younger knights in the service of older ones. The typical student when he became a bachelor was about nineteen years old.

University students were a motley group of old and young, rich and poor. Aimless ones drifted from university to university and teacher to teacher. *Organized gangs* of wandering students roamed between universities begging and stealing as they went. Many masters encouraged their students to take work in other universities and they themselves frequently went to other institutions to enrich their experience. University education was a *male privilege* and women were not allowed often to even enter university grounds.

The teacher was one holding the degree required for membership in the faculty in which he taught. Theoretically, the number of teachers on any faculty was unlimited, since any one with the necessary degree had a *right to teach*. This is another aspect of a virtual university that has been largely lost in the modern day.

The early universities were more liberal towards new knowledge than the church universities of medieval times. Yet, they were highly traditional in many ways. Their curriculum was narrow and their methods of presenting truth highly formalized. To the discovery of methods of accumulating knowledge, they added almost nothing. They were, however, a great source for the *spread of existing knowledge* as they were centers of book trade and their students and teachers traveled widely.

Seventeenth through nineteenth Century

Largely Puritans founded Massachusetts in the early seventeenth century. To help make children Puritans, the General Court of Massachusetts ordered every town of fifty families to employ a teacher of reading and writing whose fees should be paid by the parents or by the town. The *Bible* was the chief book for children, and the other books for children were all of a religious nature. *Harvard College*, founded by the Puritans in 1636, was the first higher institution of learning in the American colonies. It was established and run by both the state and the church to supply Puritan pulpits with learned ministers and the colony with teachers and magistrates.

Early nineteenth century education was driven by the Industrial Revolution to find more efficient ways to teach larger numbers of students in a formal way. At the beginning of the nineteenth century Joseph Lancaster founded a university in a poor section of London. In order that he might extend the benefit of his teaching to as many children as possible, he hit upon the device of using older pupils as assistant teachers for the younger children (see Figure 26 "Monitorial Method"). He first taught the lesson to these *monitors*, and each of them in turn taught it to the group of children that had been placed under his control. The methods of teaching were highly oriented to memorization and rigid discipline (Duggan, 1936). With this monitorial system a single teacher was able to direct the instruction of a very large number of pupils. Lancaster himself thus cared for an entire university of 1,000 children.

In 1814 under the leadership of Lancaster a Society was formed to spread the monitorial teaching method in England. The *Anglican Church* feared the non-sectarian teachings of these monitorial universities and developed a counter educational system that also used the monitorial method of older students teaching younger students but emphasized the teaching of religion. The educational activities made practical by the use of the monitorial method raised the interest of the public in education. Those activities were thus partly responsible for the subsequent efforts by the government to organize education in England.

Figure 26: "Monitorial Method". Five senior students or monitors are giving instructions to five classes. The junior students are assembled at the draft stations, their toes to lines cut in the floor. With pointers the senior students are giving instruction from lessons suspended from the lesson rail.

The monitorial system was introduced into the *United States* in 1806. It spread with great rapidity throughout the country. Its comparative low cost appealed to the charitable societies that were most prominent in attempting to spread education to the poor. The monitorial method was widely adopted for elementary universities and secondary universities throughout the first half of the nineteenth century in the United States.

So what happened to the monitorial method? As material wealth increased and the people became better informed about the needs of students and were willing to contribute funds to education, the *mechanical methods* that had become part of the monitorial universities were abandoned. The mechanical methods were considered inferior to the guidance of expert teachers. In universities the monitorial method is reflected in the role of graduate assistants or teaching assistants who are graduate students or senior undergraduate students. In some universities these students are solely responsible for entire classes.

Twentieth Century

In the twentieth century, the techniques of the Industrial Revolution were applied to improving the welfare of society (Boyd, 1968) Despite the huge cost of various social services, education in advanced countries usually claims a bigger share of the *gross national product* than any other investment except defense. Government-based planning commissions are commonplace, and tax-supported education dominates the general offerings of education. The First and Second World Wars brought to the fore the importance of total mobilization. This experience along with the increasing globalization of industry led to increasing specialization and organization. Much of education is now professionally provided and state guaranteed.

With the advent of radio and television, countries increased their interests in distance education. Places such as the Open University in Great Britain and National Radio Institute in the United States of America were created in the mid-nineteenth century. These institutions help students access quality teachers and information despite being bound to home or work in someplace distant from the teacher and the original source of the information. In the United States over 100,000 million Americans have used *distance education* methods during the nineteenth century.

A national sample of U.S. households was surveyed by telephone in the spring of 1995 (Dillman et al, 1995). The findings are:

- The attitudes and behavior of people from all age groups, income levels, and backgrounds indicate that a large majority of adults recognize the value of lifelong education.

- Getting educated once is not enough in our knowledge-based economy.

- Teaching only in the traditional classroom will not meet the public's demand for tailored educational services.

- No single educational approach or technique will make lifelong learning accessible to everyone, because different people face different obstacles.

- Distance education strategies have the potential to overcome significant barriers to lifelong learning.

These fascinating possibilities of technology to influence education must ironically be balanced with the *shortage of trained people* in the information technology fields. In 1997, according to the Information Technology Association of America, 190,000 information technology jobs are vacant across the United States, and a prediction by the U.S. Department of Labor indicates that new and expanding technologies will account for 80 percent of new jobs between 1997 and 2007. The opportunities to juxtapose the need for information technology training with the tools of information technology are many.

Libraries and the Internet

Throughout history the *information explosion* has been perceived as outstripping people's ability to manage information. One partial solution has been to build archives of documents. Egyptian documents such as the *Book of the Dead* were so important that already several hundred years before the birth of Christ, the Egyptians had a library for such books in Alexandria.

Bibliographies are pointers or links to documents. Simple *bibliographies* were published in the Middle Ages. By the 1700s, scholars had prepared bibliographies exhibiting a variety of approaches both by author and subject. In his annual report for 1851, the Secretary of the Smithsonian Institution in the United States called attention to the fact that

> about twenty thousand volumes…purporting to be additions to the sum of human knowledge, are published annually; and unless this mass be properly arranged, and the means furnished by which its contents may be ascertained, literature and science will be overwhelmed by their own unwieldy bulk.

This fear of being overwhelmed by the explosion of information is a recurring theme of modern civilization.

The *National Library of Medicine* built the first large-volume, computerized bibliographic retrieval system in the 1960s. To obtain citations a health professional first conveyed an information need to a search intermediary at the National Library of Medicine, Maryland, USA. The search intermediary then formulated an online query, and a list of relevant citations was then printed and mailed to the health professional. The turn-around time was one month. In the 1990s this system was made accessible to the world through the Web for free with instant access to its ten million documents. There are hundreds of bibliographic retrieval systems storing hundreds of *millions of citations* and receiving millions of queries each year (Hall and Brown, 1983).

In the United States in 1969 the Advanced Research Projects Agency (ARPA) demonstrated the viability of the first Internet Protocol computer network called ARPAnet. The original motivation for development was resource sharing, as ARPA noticed many contractors were tending to request the same resources. Researchers almost immediately began using the ARPAnet for collaboration through electronic mail and other services. The high utility of the network led people to want increased connectivity. Many organizations in which these networks were placed wanted to connect the ARPAnet to their local network so that each user of the local area network would also through that network have access to the ARPAnet. By now the Internet is all the networks using the Internet Protocol that cooperate to form a seamless network for their collective users (Krol, 1992).

Any one company does not own the Internet. Instead everyone owns and pays for their own part. A college or corporation pays for its connection to some regional network, which in turn pays a national provider for access. This arrangement is somewhat like the international telephone network.

Internet growth has been phenomenal. While the Internet was originally developed for research-related purposes, by May 1994 commercial users had exceeded 50 percent of the connected base and commercial usage was growing most rapidly. The number of Internet hosts is increasing at an exponential number with no apparent immediate limiting factor (NGI, 2000).

The Internet has been used in education from its early days. In disciplines, such as computer science, where teachers and students routinely access the Internet, email has been used for communicating between teacher and student since the 1960s. However, the Internet alone was not useful enough to most disciplines to have much impact on education. It was the wide-spread of an application that rides on the Internet that led to the major impact of the Internet in education. This application is the World Wide Web.

The World Wide Web began at the European Particle Physics Laboratory in Geneva, Switzerland about 1990. There, scientists collaborate with many other scientists around the world on the subject of high-energy physics, and the Web was developed to facilitate electronic collaboration (Berners-Lee et al. 1994). Since the first Web browser was developed, many browsers are freely available.

The strength of the Web is based on two simple standards:

- one for structuring document (HTML) and
- the other for addresses (URLs) for those documents on the Internet.

These standards have become universally accepted and form the basis for a vast, new library of largely un-indexed but freely available information. The Web provides an accessible and rich source of documents for university faculty and students.

The cost of physical libraries is substantial. First there is the space to house the collection and second there is the cost of the physical product itself (see Figure 27 "Library"). Increasingly, users are relying on the Web for information that otherwise might have been obtained exclusively via a physical library. Such developments have ramifications for budgeting, staffing, and other aspects of running a university.

Figure 27: "Library". These three photos show the central library at the University of Maryland, Baltimore County, USA from the outside and inside. The building is a massive physical structure and houses an expensive paper collection. Many people in the library spend significant time in front of computer screens.

Delivering Degrees

What have universities been doing by way of delivering education, particularly degrees online? What patterns does one observe? What plans do the universities have?

Distance Education Survey

A survey on distance education courses offered by American higher education institutions was initiated by the U.S. Department of Education in 1995 (National, 1997). A third of higher education institutions offered distance education courses, and another quarter planned to offer such courses. In 1995, US higher education institutions provided 26,000 *distance education courses* to 800,000 students.

Distance education courses were delivered by *two-way interactive video* at 60 percent and by one-way pre-recorded video at 50 percent of the institutions. About a quarter of the institutions used the Internet to deliver their distance education courses. About a quarter of the institutions that offered distance education courses offered degrees that students could complete by taking distance education courses exclusively. In 1995 there were approximately 1,000 degrees and 200 certificates offered that students could receive by taking distance education courses exclusively.

Trends by Discipline

To look into *patterns of Web activity* across universities and to explore more systematically the factors affecting such patterns, the content of the Web itself has been analyzed. *Analysts* were told to begin at a university home page and to work from there to find courses. Across American universities, the top 6 programs by Web activity, in descending order were:

1. Computer and Information Engineering
2. Engineering
3. Life Sciences
4. Physical Sciences
5. Business Management
6. Agricultural Sciences.

These 6 programs accounted for 60 percent of the Web activity.

Technologically sophisticated programs, such as computer science and engineering, dominated the Web. One might have guessed that those programs that most use computers would be the most likely to exploit the Web in delivering education. This is consistent with the theory that successful innovation must *fit into the workflow*. Those in the technologically sophisticated disciplines are more likely to be comfortable with the use of the Web in education.

Trends by Date

The annual Campus Computing Survey is a large continuing study of the role of information technology in US higher education. Each year more than 600 two-and four-year public and private colleges and universities participate in this survey, which focuses on campus planning and policy affecting the role of information technology in teaching, learning, and scholarship (Green, 1999).

The 1999 survey data reveal that more college courses are using more technology resources. Over half of all college courses make use of electronic mail, up from 40 percent in 1998 and 20 percent in 1995. Similarly, the percentage of college courses using Web resources in the syllabus rose from 10 in 1995 and 30 percent in 1998 to 40 percent in 1999.

More than two-thirds of the institutions in the 1999 survey provide online undergraduate applications on their Web sites, up from one-half in 1998. Three-fourths make the course catalog available online, compared to two-thirds in 1998. Library-based course reserves readings are available on the Web at one-fourth of the institutions. At this rate of growth one might predict that online undergraduate applications, online catalogs, and similar services will be available at essentially all universities in the near future.

An Online Degree

Dozens of masters degrees in information technology-related disciplines are now available on the Internet. *Southwest Missouri State University, USA,* offers a virtual mode Master's Degree in Computer Information Systems. The advertisement says (Southwest, 2000):

> The Master of Science in Computer Information Systems program at Southwest Missouri State University, USA is clearly an idea whose time has come. It meets the needs of the non-traditional student by combining minimal on campus instruction time with extensive distance learning via the Internet. This program is designed to work with the schedules and careers of today's busy professionals.

The degree is available largely online but does involve four weeklong meetings. One such meeting occurs every six months during the two-year program. Following the *one-week meeting*, learning continues off campus in virtual mode and communication is largely via email. Accrediting bodies tend to require fairly traditional, face-to-face education. The weeklong, face-to-face meetings help satisfy accrediting requirements.

Before acceptance into the program, students are required to supply *letters of support* from their employer that assures the university that the employer expects the student to commit substantial time to the two-year degree program. While this approach might be seen to discourage some students from applying, the marketing experience also suggests that such requirements attract students and employers who are committed to the program, and thus build the quality reputation of the program.

By 1999, two cohorts of 20 students each had finished their online Master's Degrees at Southwest Missouri State University. The stories and photos of each of the graduated students can be found on the University Web site. The program has earned high reviews from various sources (Fryer, 1999).

Open University

Harold Wilson, the former Prime Minister of *Great Britain*, launched the idea of a 'University of the Air' in 1963. In 2000 the Open University is *Britain's largest educational and training organization.* It leads the world in the large-scale application of technology to learning (Daniel, 1998). There are two essential characteristics that make the Open University different from most other universities:

- It is open to any adult living in the European Union, irrespective of previous educational qualifications.

- Teaching materials are delivered to the students in their own homes or places of work—by post, by computer, and via national television broadcasts. Tutors provide local support.

The Open University awards B.A. and B.Sc. degrees, MA, MS, a M.B.A, a Ph.D., and numerous certificates.

The median age for graduating students is in the mid-thirties. The Open University also operates in *countries* around the world. Degrees have been awarded to over *180,000 students*.

Total cost of study to British students to include tuition fees, residential university fees, travel, postage, books and materials, over the appropriate number of courses and years of study to receive a degree is about $6,000. In a typical American state university, *tuition fees* for a degree might be expected to be about $20,000.

Open University employs about 12,000 people (Open, 2000). Fewer than 1,000 employees are academics per se. About 8,000 are tutorial staff or teaching assistants. The university has an annual budget of about $300 million. About 60 percent of this is from the government and most of the rest from tuition fees. The expenditures include 30 percent to academic costs, 25 percent to support for tutoring, and 20 percent for courseware production. This emphasis on *production costs* would not be seen in typical universities where teachers use existing textbooks. The Open University has such a large enrollment that it can afford to invest heavily in tailored products to serve its students' needs.

Studying a conventional Open University course involves *supported distance learning*. This means that students are at home in their own time using custom designed paper-based study materials and where appropriate home experiment kits, television broadcasts or video tapes, audio tapes, and other media and equipment appropriate to a particular course. It also means that the student has an individual tutor assigned for the duration of the course. This tutor will provide advice over the telephone, via letters, and at live tutorials at a local study center. In addition, the tutor makes detailed comments on each 'Tutor Marked Assignment' that with the final examination grade form the student's grade on the course.

Courses presented via the Internet normally have the paper-based materials, any audio/video tapes and home experiment kits sent via conventional surface mail before the course begins, although some course material may also be available in electronic form. The minimum requirement to participate in a course is that the student must be able to send and receive Internet *email messages* and be able to attach files to these messages. The student may write his assignments using any major word processor. The marked assignment is returned to the student as a Microsoft Word file attached to an email message.

University of Maryland, College Park, USA

The University of Maryland at College Park, USA, began in 1947 a branch called the called the College of Special and Continuation Studies. The focus was on helping educate people who had returned from the Second World War and needed special educational opportunities. In 1949, the US military solicited proposals from American universities to develop and deliver degree programs to US soldiers in the occupation forces in Europe. The College of Special and Continuation Studies was the only respondent to the solicitation, won the contract, and in 1949 seven faculties flew from the USA to Germany to begin work in the educational programs for US soldiers in Europe. In 1959 the name was changed to University College, and in 1970 it became a separately accredited institution and assumed the name University of Maryland University College (UMUC).

Since 1947 UMUC has ambitiously expanded its offerings to American military bases around the world. The university maintains classrooms at military bases in Asia, Europe, and other continents. These programs were fairly traditional in mode of delivery but have increasingly moved to distance education and now online format. In 1959 UMUC taught its first course via TV. In 1972 UMUC began distance education programs modeled after the British Open University programs. In 1993 UMUC launched its virtual university with courses for a bachelor's degree available online. In 1997 UMUC launched its first online graduate degree, a M.S. in Computer Systems Management.

UMUC has awarded over one hundred thousand degrees and has enrolled about 3 million students (UMUC, 2000). As of the year 2000, about half of its educational activity was occurring online. About one-third of UMUC students live in the USA, about one-third in Europe, and about one-third in Asia. About 70 percent of its revenue comes from tuition and about 70 percent of its cost goes to instruction.

In December 1999 UMUC became the first public university in the USA to launch a for-profit company to market its online courses. UMUC wants to be the world leader in online education and feels that dealing appropriately with global companies as providers of students requires the flexibility that a private company has. Several tens of millions of dollars of venture capital are being recruited and in a few years the company is intended to sell shares publicly (Katz-Stone, 2000).

Running a University

Universities have certain basic functions and structures. The function is to educate students. The structures include course material and classrooms. Teachers, students, and administrators work together. How do they change across time? One important structure for change is money – how is that managed in universities? How is quality assured for university activities? Answers to these questions are a pre-requisite to being able to run universities and continually improve them.

A Model of Change

The change process in an educational organization has been extensively studied. There is general agreement that three phases of the change over time can be identified. Typically, these are called an initiation phase, an implementation phase, and an institutionalization phase (Fullan, 1991). The initiation phase involves many processes and dynamics leading to the decision that a certain change target will be chosen. After the change is initiated, the implementation phase evolves, often as a series of experiments tested in practice relating to the change target. In the institutional phase, the change is no longer at the experimental level but is integrated into the mainstream operations of the institution. It has been estimated that movement from initiation through implementation to institutionalization with respect to a technological innovation in an educational institution can be expected to be something like a five-year process and thus overall success cannot quickly be expected.

The linearity of the process is not as direct as these three phases would indicate. Within any innovation, there will be many sub-innovations, some of which will only be at the initiation phase while others may be in the institutionalization phase. The success of early sub-innovations (success being defined as full institutionalization) can be taken as a partial indicator of the likelihood of the full change being successful. Conversely, the lack of success of early sub-innovations should be taken as a warning. The initiation phase has a major effect on what follows, and thus the factors that influence an organization to commit itself to involvement in the initiation phase, to start a change process or not, are of particular importance.

While the change phases provide one dimension for studying the change process relating to a technological innovation in an educational institution, what makes the change process concrete are entities that relate specifically to what happens in practice. Twelve change entities can be briefly described as follows (Collis and DeBoer, 2000):

- The *educational target* should not be the use of possible techniques, but the techniques should serve the educational changes that are to be initiated, such as higher quality learning in the new students.

- The willingness to re-allocate funds is not only a necessary strategy if technology-based teaching is to become a core part of a university's operation, it is also a measure of the level of commitment to the concept by different organizational units (Bates, 1997). The management should therefore also acknowledge that change will take time and will require financing through this time, reflected in the change entity *budget*.

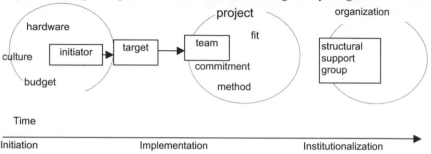

Figure 28: "Model of Change in Universities". This model shows the transition from initiation, implementation, to institutionalization. Only some of the entities are shown. Adapted from Boer and Collins (2000).

- Another change entity of importance is the receptivity of the organization to change and innovation in general. An *innovative culture* is thus another change entity.

- Intersecting the dimensions of culture, organization, and methodology is the entity relating to the basic style of the change process: *bottom-up or top-down*, or a combination of both.

- Change entities relating to *Software that is bought or built* and *Quality hardware and network* relate to medium quality.

- It is important that the innovation can adapt to the way that an individual instructor wants to work, even as the instructor too will need to make some adaptation in his or her typical teaching practices. The extent to which it takes the instructor time and energy to make the change is a useful index for the amount of resistance that will occur to the change. *Fit with instructional practices* is therefore an important change entity directly related to the entity educational target.

- The *initiation target* that started the change process is also a change entity. In the initiation phase, certain persons start certain processes, so that the organization starts thinking about the change. A relatively small number of enthusiasts and early adopters should extend the implementation to the main body of the teaching force. These *key figures to initiate* can be seen as an important change entity because they must make clear the goal of the change. They are also the persons who could initiate the sub-innovation of a social learning environment in the institution, so that colleagues could benefit from the experiences of others (House, 1974).

- To successfully move from the initiation phase to the implementation phase, some entities that were important in the initiation phase will remain important and others will emerge. A *Project Team* needs to be formed for the implementation phase and must work both responsively and proactively to coordinate and lead all the on-going activities.

- When, after a few (successful) years, the organization decides to continue the change but as part of the normal and on-going practices in the organization, the change is in fact no longer a change but has been institutionalized. In this phase, where **Embedding of Use** is occurring, a **Structural Support Group** needs to be formed to support normal use of the system. In the case where the change has to be financed by external funding an institution may find it difficult to continue with the change.

It is challenging when some aspects of a change process are at the institutionalization phase and others are still at the implementation or even initiation phase. Then the same team and leadership will be called on to fulfill roles with different demands and requiring different skills (Collis and Moonen, 1994). This may be one of the major challenges in the overall change process.

Budgets

Items to consider in running or changing a university, such as culture, commitment, and team, are difficult to handle quantitatively. However, the budget is clearly quantitative, precise, and readily manipulated. What is known about budgets in universities?

A virtual educational organization in the sense of this book focuses on education rather than research or service. However, an interesting perspective on the scope of a university budget comes from looking at the budget of a major research university. The modern *research university* is a complex, international conglomerate of highly diverse businesses. The University of Michigan, USA, for example, has an annual budget of more than \$2.5 billion. If it were a private company, then the University of Michigan would rank roughly 200th on the Fortune 500 list of largest companies in the U.S.A. (Duderstadt, 1995). The large research university may be seen as operating as a holding company for thousands of faculty entrepreneurs. The faculty has teaching duties, but performance in these teaching duties is only modestly linked to salary. This model of research universities does not apply to community colleges.

The revenue theory of cost is appropriate for describing research universities (Bowen, 1980). In this theory, a university gets as much money each year as it can, spends all that money that year, and next year operates in the same way. From universities of similar standard in the United States the amount of money spent to educate a student can differ by a factor of two and still the quality of education has not been demonstrated to be affected. Bowen's conclusions include (page 227):

> If one observed strong central tendencies toward certain levels of cost, or found clear modalities in the way higher education is conducted, or could discover definite relationships between costs and educational outcomes, then one might find empirical support for particular recommendations. Unfortunately, the study of institutions did not reveal such clear-cut conclusions...Instead, the dispersion of costs proved to be so wide, even for ostensibly similar institutions, that the mode cannot be assumed to represent an ideal or widely accepted standard. This variance is of course consistent with the revenue theory of cost, namely, that the cost of any institution is largely determined by the amount of revenue it can raise.

The revenue theory of cost for universities means (ibid., page 15) that:

> When resources are increased, they find uses for the new funds, and unit costs go up. When resources are decreased, they express keen regret and they protest, but in the end they accept the inevitable and unit costs go down. This set of generalizations might be called the revenue theory of costs.

As one goes from public research universities to teaching community colleges, one sees something closer to an accounting model in which revenue is related to costs.

What is an accounting model for a teaching organization? Most states allocate funds to *community colleges* on the basis of enrollment. A funding unit is the smallest unit that corresponds to a unit of student load and is the product of an educational organization (Bibby, 1983). The instructional workforce consists of faculty and can be measured by the number of full-time equivalent faculty. Productivity is equal to the number of funding units divided by the number of full-time equivalent faculty.

Time studies of community college teachers indicate weekly hours for classroom function (Adams, 1976):

T = weekly hours for classroom function,

x = weekly hours in the classroom or laboratory, and

y = number of students taught.

The formula says that $T = x + (.7) x + (.08) y$. The term $.7x$ represents preparation time and $.08y$ represents the time spent evaluating students. For example, a faculty member teaching 15 hours per week with a student load of 150 will spend $15 + .7(15) + .08(150) = 37.5$ weekly hours for classroom functions alone. The difference between the activities of a teacher/lecturer in a community or teaching college and the activities of a professor in a research university are dramatic. At some research universities a university lecturer teaches one course a semester, whereas at some community colleges the lecturer teaches five times that much.

These accounting models can facilitate tracking the impact of online education on faculty costs. Furthermore, if financial incentives for faculty to participate in online education could be determined, then faculty would more readily contribute to online education.

The accounting model is useful to guide the distribution of resources. The model of teacher costs is part of that. More generally, the university needs to distribute money across departments or centers. Some departments are primarily involved in teaching, while other departments, such as computing services and library, provide support to the teaching departments. Can one rationalize the distribution of money across departments and enlist the aid of computers in managing these distributions?

The typical approach to public agency budgeting in the past has been to pool most income centrally and to approach expenditure budgeting without regard to which units or activities generated the income. Thus, units and individuals see no relationship between their income generating activities and the budgets available to them. *Budget-centered management* attempts to identify the revenues associated with each budget center and return those revenues to that unit while charging each center, as nearly as possible, with the expenses associated with its activities (Nelson and Scoby, 1998).

Budget-centered management creates management, budgetary, and reward structures that tie resources to performance closely enough so that individuals will see how their own actions influence the security and fiscal-well being of their units and themselves (OPA, 1996). Other desired results include:

- integrating and coordinating academic and fiscal planning,
- flattening the management structure and further decentralizing decision making (expenditure decisions will be made closer to the point of service delivery),
- matching costs more clearly with benefits,
- providing members of the community with a stronger sense of the relationship between performance and rewards, and
- subjecting service units to scrutiny for efficiency, effectiveness, and proper incentives.

The rational for budget centers is that a unit can increase its performance and earn reward proportional to its achievement.

The base funding for state-supported universities in the USA may be delivered for reasons other than educational performance. When the state economy is strong and taxes plentiful, the universities get more funds. For instance, the state of Maryland, USA experienced a budget surplus in 1999, and the state governor announced (Glendenning, 1999): "Our ambitious $1.23 billion investment in capital construction, expansion, and renovation will benefit virtually every Maryland higher education institution and will provide a brighter future to every college student in the State." What is one reason why this money would go into construction rather than into information technology or staff for information technology? Because the state surplus is unpredictable and construction costs are one time whereas staff costs are recurrent.

When the state budget is less than predicted, higher education institutions, independent of their educational performance, may get less revenue. This environment of the university may reflect itself in the values and objectives of the university and would need to be taken into consideration when deciding what units had made what contributions to the objectives of the university. The more explicit the formulas for reward relative to performance, the more easily the computer can play a positive supporting role in the running of the university by *semi-automating decisions*.

Most campuses have information technology development programs and campus support centers to assist faculty in bringing technology resources into their courses. However, very few have a formal, institutional program to recognize and reward the use of information technology as part of the faculty review process. According to Green (1999):

> Campuses continue to send mixed messages about faculty investments in information technology. Recognition and reward remain essential yet widely ignored components of technology planning at most institutions: investing in technology may put you at professional risk when departments review faculty portfolios. Failing to recognize and promote faculty who invest in technology in their scholarly and instructional activities sends a chilling message about the real departmental and institutional commitment to the integration of technology in instruction and scholarship.

The factors that will drive consistent change across a university as regards the systematic use of information technology remain to be clearly identified.

According to the Campus Computing Survey in the USA (Green, 1999), forty percent of the institutions participating in the 1999 survey identify instructional integration as their single most significant information technology challenge. Providing adequate user support ranks second among the survey respondents as the most significant challenge for their institutions. However, systematic methods for financing user support or motivating integration of technology into instruction are not widely agreed.

One Web-based service that appears late arriving in higher education is electronic commerce: only five percent of the institutions participating in the 1999 Campus Computing Survey report e-commerce capacity via their campus Web sites. Only four percent of universities report that they have a strategic plan for electronic commerce. Universities have been slow to develop a capacity for electronic commerce, and this is consistent with the relative confusion about financial models for running universities.

Unbundling the Product

Information technology may allow educational providers to separate some key functions traditionally bundled together (Massy and Zemsky, 1995). For example, not all faculty need be lecturers as more lectures become available online. The investments in knowledge codification, delivery systems, and assessment techniques may decouple the provision of learning from the certification of mastery, thus opening new modes of educational delivery.

These separations could allow colleges, universities, and other educational providers to *unbundle their offerings* and prices. Students would be able to pay for instruction with little mentoring or, alternatively, much mentoring, as they choose. They would be able to get learning with certification or contract for learning and certification separately.

What are some of the roles most vital for education online? Key roles include:

1. The technical role maintains the Internet services and deals with problems that anyone has with the hardware or software responding incorrectly.

2. The social role supports students in interacting with one another, getting to know the way of working, and any other social issues that may relate to the education.

3. The content provider determines what material is to be studied by students and how they will get access to that material.

4. The task generator assigns exercises to students.

5. The assessor evaluates the submitted exercises of students.

6. The quality controller checks whether students are satisfied with the educational experience and whether the university operates consistently

7. with its objectives.

Given adequate instructions, the social facilitator, the assessor, and the quality control roles can be assumed by part-time students. The technical role requires the kind of person who would normally operate an information technology help desk. The supplier of the technology is responsible for serious faults with the technology through maintenance contracts.

The role of content provider and task generator could be performed just once for multiple offerings of the same course. Developing new content is a separate problem from delivering education. Usually the developer of new content markets to a much larger audience than that served by a single lecturer.

The overall cost to the educational program of a systematic approach to monitoring student satisfaction and of nurturing students can be low when done by low-level staff and by computer programs. The teacher can focus on the content and pedagogy strategies. Sending multiple support staff to the physical classroom is an inefficient use of the time of most of them. However, in the asynchronous, virtual mode classroom the support staff can become involved when, and only when, they are needed.

In fall 1999 about 1,000 students enrolled in an online degree program that exhibited a successful diversification of roles as follows:

- A technical staff role (filled by several people part-time) dealt with specific user problems both from students and faculty about the technology.
- A quality control role (filled by a faculty member and a clerk) reviewed the results of student satisfaction surveys that were completed on a weekly basis by all students. Students who failed to complete the survey or who indicated vague problems were contacted by phone by the clerk.
- Teaching assistants monitored the activities of students to assure that they were doing their assigned work.
- The teacher monitored the quality of the performed work of students and the overall running of the course.

The computer tracked by user name and date every file visited. Thus one can not only determine automatically what students were actively visiting what files but also what faculty and staff had done what. Various computer programs were used to facilitate the management of the degree program.

Quality Control

Sam Walton ran an empire of *Wal-Mart* stores with a vision of reducing prices and making accessible to more customers more quality retail products. Some educational organizations have the same high-level objectives of Wal-Mart. Might universities improve the quality of educational outcomes for students, increase access to education for students, and simultaneously reduce per student costs (see Figure 29 "Mission of Organization")? These are goals of quality management, and technology can help.

The pre-eminent standard in the area of quality management is produced by the International Standards Organization and is called ISO 9000. The challenge to the organization is to invest in the additional workload of the maintenance of records for monitoring quality in such a way that the profitability of the company is improved.

Criterion	Change
quantity of customers	⬆
quality to customer	⬆
cost per customer	⬇

Figure 29: "Mission of Organization". The column on the left gives attributes of performance. The column on the right shows the desired direction of change in those attribute values; an upward-pointing arrow means 'increase' and a downward-pointing arrow means 'decrease'.

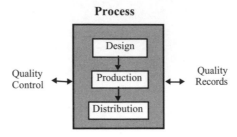

Figure 30: "Quality Control". The rectangle in the middle shows the basic process of the company. The quality records that are indicated in the right must reflect each step of the basic process. The quality control is indicated on the left and applies to the quality records relative to the ongoing company process.

One way to model the coverage of ISO 9000 is to think of the organization's operating process, its quality records, and its quality control. The operating process creates the final product or service (see Figure 30 "Quality Control"). The quality records are maintained relative to this process, and the control system corrects for divergences from quality. Quality control is supported by a procedure manual that provides guidance for the implementation of the quality system on a day-to-day basis. The control system must include a means for identifying, collecting, indexing, storing, retrieving, and maintaining quality records. The quality system must help people work to quality (Huyink and Westover, 1994). This requires both that the documentation is relevant to the standard and that the behavior of people is relevant to the standard (see Figure 31 "Documents and Behavior").

ISO 9000 is important in the first instance because it gives organizations some guidance on how to manage for quality. Secondly, mechanisms exist by which an organization can be certified for conforming to ISO 9000 specifications. With this certification in hand, an organization can better sell its product or service to its customer. It can say that the product or service is the result of a process that continually tested for quality.

In 1994 the *University of Wolverhampton* in Great Britain gained ISO 9000 certification for its core activities (Storey, 1994). This is the design and delivery of learning experiences with provision for research and consultancy services. Achieving this registered quality status represented the culmination of three years of a university-wide effort involving a small core team of missionaries, the university's quality assurance unit, and staff at all managerial and functional levels. The main goal was to provide a rational and documented base for the pursuit of quality in a large and complex university. The Chief Executive of the University of Wolverhampton said (Harrison, 1997):

> We, the staff of the University of Wolverhampton, are committed to providing high quality services regionally, nationally and internationally – to our wide range of students and other clients regardless of their gender, creed or nationality. This provision is aimed at developing the relevant knowledge, skills and competences to meet the future needs of industry, commerce and society. We will foster a cost-effective do-it-right-first-time culture by understanding and conforming to the requirements of the University's Quality system at all times.

The standard of administrative services and academic delivery has risen since the University began its effort to be ISO 9000 compliant.

The process undertaken by the University of Wolverhampton addresses the routine running of an otherwise traditional university. Successfully monitoring behavior is integral to being ISO 9000 compliant but is more generally vital to virtual education activities. Many universities are endeavoring to deliver course material in self-paced, interactive multimedia modules. The faculty at the universities are concerned that they do not have the tools or training to produce or manage such a new curriculum. Accordingly, universities are attempting to define standards for teaching loads that will take into account the technological component of a course. Surveys have been undertaken to analyze and summarize the number of hours and kinds of effort faculty have expended to prepare and teach new technology-enhanced classes. On the basis of this analysis, faculty, unit heads, and staff who have been associated with course delivery in some way define the equivalent *teaching loads* for their particular units. Relevant variables include whether faculty must learn new multimedia teaching techniques; develop their own course materials; or meet face-to-face with classes. As such standards are developed, they become integral parts of the quality management of the university.

Another model of quality in education is the Baldrige National Quality Program from the American National Institute for Standards and Technology (NIST, 1999). This program for many years only recognized business quality but in 1999 added a category for educational institutions. The quality criteria are in the following seven topics:

1. Leadership

2. Strategic Planning

3. Student and Stakeholder Focus

4. Information and Analysis

5. Faculty and Staff Focus

Mapping Documents and Behavior			
	Documents		
		Good	Bad
Behavior	Good	documents conform to standard and people follow documents	documents do not follow standards but people follow documents
	Bad	documents conform to standard but people do not	documents do not follow the standard or are missing and people do not follow them

Figure 31: "Documents and Behavior". This 4 x 4 table has columns which indicate the quality of the documents and rows which indicate the behavior of people relative to the documents.

6. Educational and Support Process Management

7. University Performance Results.

A university submits an application to the Quality Program and is judged for the extent to which it documents striving for excellence in the seven categories. The winning programs are honored in ceremonies attended by the President of the United States.

Earning ISO 9000 certification or a Baldrige Quality Award is a kind of accreditation. Accreditation is a rich and important facet of university life (USDE, 2000). A higher education organization that wants accreditation may approach a *wide range of organizations* to accredit its services. For instance, Indiana University Southeast says (IUS, 2000):

> Indiana University Southeast is fully accredited by the North Central Association of Colleges and Secondary Universities, by the American Assembly of Collegiate Universities of Business, by the National League for Nursing, by the Indiana State Board of Education, by the National Council for Accreditation of Teacher Education, and by the Indiana State Board of Nurses' Registration and Nursing Education.

From this list one sees one sample of organizations that have granted accreditation.

The *Distance Education and Training Council* is unique in American accreditation because it is based upon a method of instruction rather than educational level or subject matter discipline (DETC, 2000). It covers all programs, courses and distance study endeavors of an institution, including degree, non-degree, vocational and avocational programs. Unlike regional or specialized accrediting agencies, the Accrediting Commission of the Distance Education and Training Council provides distance education institutions with a single source of national recognition.

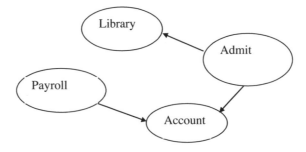

Figure 32: "Centralized, Monolithic Approach". Relations among information system components. The arrows show the flow of information from a student admitted to accounting where fees are collected.

The process of accreditation begins when a bona fide distance education institution with two years of operating experience voluntarily sends an *Application for Accreditation* to the Distance Education and Training Council offices. The review requires an in-depth self-evaluation report; review of all courses by subject matter experts; survey of students, graduates, state departments of education, federal agencies, Better Business Bureaus, and other official bodies; and an on-site inspection to verify information. The Accrediting Commission then reviews all reports and surveys in terms of the published standards and determines whether or not to accredit the institution. Only about one in four institutions applying for accreditation become accredited. If an institution is accredited, it must conform to all educational and business standards of the Distance Education and Training Council's Accrediting Commission, submit annual reports, and be re-examined every five years. In addition, subject matter experts must send any new course developed by an institution to the Commission for review.

Producing University Information Systems

All universities whether operating in virtual mode or traditional mode have certain common functions. Students register for courses, teachers guide the learning of students, and students graduate with certain credentials. Administrators have the challenge to guide their institutions to the selection of the appropriate information technology tools. Some universities opt to build their own systems from scratch, but most purchase systems from commercial sources and then tailor the product to their particular university's needs.

Generations

The first generation of education information systems was mainly concerned with administrative and accounting issues, i.e. payroll, enrollment, general ledger, and was structured as a set of batch procedures, highly proprietary and with very limited capabilities of exchanging data (see Figure 32 "Centralized, Monolithic Approach"). With the second generation of information systems, the scope was extended to the support of a limited set of activities, mainly registration and some information services, related to the student. The concept of integration between procedures was introduced, with the aim of improving the effectiveness of the overall organization and individual units, through a better exploitation of the integrated information history available in the education organization.

The third generation puts the focus on the student needs and professional aspects, in order to construct, incrementally, a homogeneous and consistent set of information. The objective is to evolve from isolated support to the individual units to the optimization of the cycle of activities related to the education of the student. Thus, the structure of the information system has changed from a set of autonomous fragmented procedures, first generation, to a closed proprietary block of functions, second generation, up to the modular, distributed and open environment which represents the objective of the third generation of information systems. Such modularity and openness supports a marketplace that evolves quickly and better supports educators and students. Individual products may be selected, evolved, and maintained independently even by different suppliers.

Different University Needs

Different universities have different *requirements*. The Education Network of Maine, USA does distance learning with no residential students and needs support for such distant students. The Maricopa Community Colleges, USA have a commuter base with diverse needs. The University of Texas at Austin, USA has a large, residential student population. These different universities have different information technology needs.

There are eight academic units in the University of Maine System, seven traditional campuses and the *Education Network of Maine* (ENM). ENM supports the distance learning programs of the University System. To understand the needs of a distant student, the University developed scenarios for a student enrolling in courses from separate University of Maine System campuses. Several scenarios for those fictional students follow their progress through a maze of campus procedures. The conclusion was that unless enrollment and administrative services were

Figure 33: "Server Farm". This university central computing facility houses the servers and mass-storage facilities for the main campus computing.

reconfigured for ENM students the process would be discouraging. Telecommunications and technology have done more than link people together at a distance; they have also revealed that traditional processes for serving them are not particularly suited to an integrated, virtual mode of operation.

The *Maricopa County Community College District* (MCCCD) in Arizona is the United States' second-largest system of its kind, exceeded only by the Los Angeles system. It offers 6,000 courses to a population of commuter students. MCCCD has problems not unrelated to those identified by ENM – namely, MCCCD needs to facilitate the movement of students to and from its various operations. To develop the information technology infrastructure to support its educational mission, MCCCD contracted with a major software company to develop a Learner Centered System. This Learner Centered System replaced, integrated, and expanded the functionality of MCCCD's previous systems that impacted learners, such as the Student Information System, the Monitoring Academic Progress System, the Course Program Register, the Course Inventory Audit, the tutor management system, and the on-line grading system.

The *University of Texas at Austin* has evolved its computing system over several decades, adding technological innovations as appropriate. The university licenses software from established companies that service the education sector. However, the university's systems are generally programmed in-house. The university employs about 400 full-time computer programmers.

The computational needs and costs are radically different depending on the type and size of a university. The University of Texas at Austin has 50,000 students and its information systems are not applicable to a smaller university. For a small university, such as the *University of Texas at Permian Basin* with 1,000 students, the university's accounting needs can be adequately handled with a spreadsheet package on a personal computer. The *University of Vermont* with its 10,000 students is intermediate in size between the University of Texas at Austin and the University of Texas at Permian Basin. The University of Vermont employs 50 full-time information technology staff and licenses its main information system from a commercial vendor. In addition to staffing costs are, of course, hardware and software costs, and mid-sized universities, such as the University of Vermont, will have central facilities with servers and storage devices that fill a large room (see Figure 33 "Server Farm").

The *Tennessee Board of Regents* serves approximately 200,000 students and is committed to connecting students and services so that every student is assured online, immediate access to admissions, registration, and grading information. The Tennessee Board of Regents has contracted with one software house for all its software needs and that software house is described next.

All Purpose

A university that wants an integrated information technology system faces a large challenge when it wants to implement this system from scratch in-house. Why not purchase a system from a company with expertise in providing such solutions for universities? One of many vendors is *Systems & Computer Technology Corporation* (SCT, 2000).

The University of Texas at Austin uses SCT software. The University of Vermont paid SCT one million dollars for a license to its major university information system and assigns five full-time staff in-house to maintain the operation of that SCT system. The multi-year contract that the Tennessee Board of Regents signed with a commercial vendor is a contract with SCT for installation of SCT software throughout the state of Tennessee.

One of SCT's major products for higher education is called Banner. Banner enables an educational enterprise to operate based on a common set of business practices: Manage the Enterprise, Forecast to Enroll, Matriculate to Educate, and Plan to Fund (see Figure 34" "Education Business Practices"). University users manage revenue and costs with processing designed specifically for the higher education environment. Managing the workforce goes beyond payroll, employment, compensation, and benefits. Position control, tenure, deferred pay, work-study, and regulatory requirements further define the information needs. Banner's enterprise model supports core financial and human resources business processes with built-in workflow, centralized or distributed information processing, decision support, and employee self-service. Potential students access the institution's information, apply, and research financial aid by themselves across the Internet. With Banner, faculty and students can advise, register, grade, and locate financial aid sources by themselves.

Through the Banner interface a students can enter their personal id and retrieve personal information or can view the university catalog of courses, the timetable, and so on (see Figure 35 "SCT Student View"). The logon screen for employees is basically the same as the logon screen for students. The faculty screen includes a menu for grades, schedules, and class lists. On selecting the "Grades" option faculty members are taken to the grade book for their classes and enter the grades and attendance data dynamically.

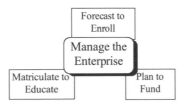

Figure: 34: "Education Business Practices". To manage the enterprise, SCT includes focuses on the three functions depicted in the plain rectangles.

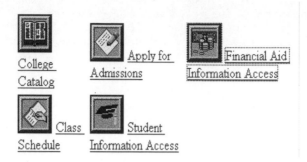

Figure 35: SCT Student View: Part of the screen as seen by a student using the SCT screen.

Limited Systems

SCT provides a system-wide, general-purpose information system for traditional higher education institutions. For virtual educational organizations, the administrator's needs may be more focused and various *specialist products* may be important to consider. For example, one product supports largely online forums and another is a course environment.

The system Connect Online provides an email and bulletin board system for universities. With *Connect Online*, the educational organization can:

- Send mail to groups using address lists.

- See when users last logged onto the system.

- Set per-document download and hourly access charges.

- Control access rights by user and by document.

5,000 universities use the Connect OnLine system to communicate electronically (Connect, 2000).

Oracle Corporation developed the *Oracle Learning Architecture* (Oracle, 2000). This Architecture supports teachers in authoring content on the Web and students in accessing the courses across the Web. The functionality includes administration, reporting, and teaching:

- The system administration features include user profile management and tracking, access security at user or course level, and user self-registration.

- Reporting supports usage statistics, user comments, broad administrative reporting, and automated royalty calculation.

- Teaching functions include customized course paths based on user competency, online access to instructors, and competency feedback via skills testing.

These three functions are key in the delivery of education.

A Historical Example

NovaNET has a longer online history than most online education activities. *PLATO* originated in the early 1960s at the University of Illinois (Woolley, 1994). Professor Don Bitzer became interested in using computers for teaching and, with some colleagues, founded the Computer-based Education Research Laboratory. Bitzer, an electrical engineer, collaborated with a few

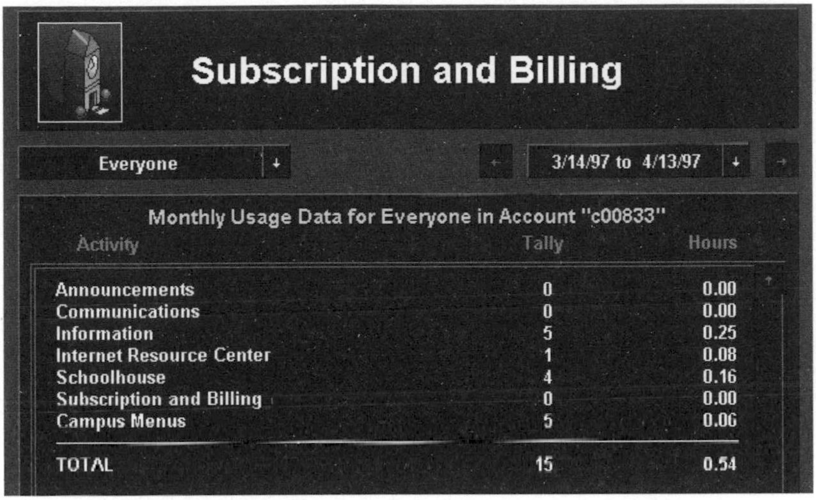

Figure 36: "NovaNET Billing". The Web interface provides detailed information for billing with activity type identified in the leftmost column and hours usage in the rightmost column.

other engineers to design the PLATO hardware. To write the software, he collected a varied staff ranging from university professors to high university students. Together they built a system that was at least a decade ahead of its time in many ways.

PLATO was one of the first timesharing systems to be operated in public. Both courseware authors and their students used high-resolution graphics display terminals, which were connected to a central mainframe. A special-purpose programming language called TUTOR was used to write educational software. This combination of timesharing system, high-resolution graphics display terminals, and the TUTOR programming language was a *landmark engineering accomplishment*.

Throughout the *1960s*, PLATO remained a small system, supporting only a single classroom of terminals. About 1972, PLATO began a transition to a new generation of mainframes that would support one thousand users simultaneously. Control Data Corporation became a principal for PLATO.

From the late 1960s and through the 1970s, the development of courseware for PLATO proceeded at an impressive rate. A large *library of courseware* for a wide range of topics, including biology, literature, and mathematics, was accumulated. The techniques were targeted to exploit the technology of the time, though they seem dated relative to the multimedia capabilities of computers in the twenty-first century.

PLATO was popular but not popular enough. As microcomputers were becoming a more cost-effective platform for education than PLATO with its mainframe-based architecture, many of the Control Data systems were closed. The revenue generated by PLATO had not been enough to merit the *costs of transforming* the tools and courses to new platforms.

NovaNET is a descendant of the PLATO project. In 1986 NovaNet Learning Incorporated was selected by the University of Illinois to operate, develop and provide an online learning environment that would among other things market the PLATO courseware library. NovaNET

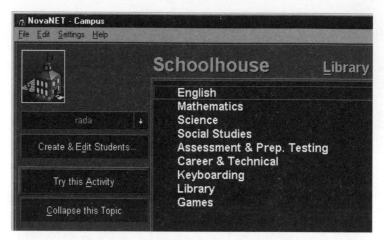

Figure 37: "Schoolhouse Window". Top half of NovaNET's Schoolhouse window.

operates in partnership with the University of Illinois but as a private, *for-profit company* (NovaNet, 2000).

NovaNET allows free use by individuals. However, organizations that want to subscribe to the NovaNET service pay various fees. The system is able to monitor the amount of time that each user spends on each feature of the NovaNET system (see Figure 36 "NovaNET Billing"). An organization can then pay based on the amount of usage.

For home use one can download the *NovaNET Campus software* for free and visit a substantial library of material. On first entering the online campus, one can select the University house icon and be taken into a set of options that are either to manage student accounts or to take courses (see Figure 37 "University Window"). The library of lessons is hierarchically sorted.

By choosing the discussion, one is taken into a discussion or *bulletin board* system on which students, teachers, and others can share ideas. This discussion system was developed in the 1980s for PLATO when such systems were not yet popular on the Internet.

NovaNet offers packaged *curricula*. Topics include fundamental skills education, high university and college subjects, life skills, study skills, job skills, vocational training, and English as a Second Language. Each curriculum is organized into a number of units.

Units are composed of:

- a diagnostic and prescriptive pre-test

- three to twelve NovaNET lessons

- a post-test to confirm mastery of unit objectives

Students begin with a pre-test that diagnoses skill deficiencies. If no deficiencies are identified, NovaNET promotes the student to the next unit. Otherwise, NovaNET recommends a customized prescription of lessons. After successfully completing the lessons, students take the post-test to ensure that they have mastered all the unit's objectives. Instructors may override the system at any point to modify the prescription, reassign *pre- and post-tests,* or advance students to the next unit.

NovaNET's *student management system* promotes individualized instruction. Instructors have a means of managing instruction and monitoring, evaluating and reporting on student progress. A menu-driven format lets instructors add and remove students and assign instruction. Assignments

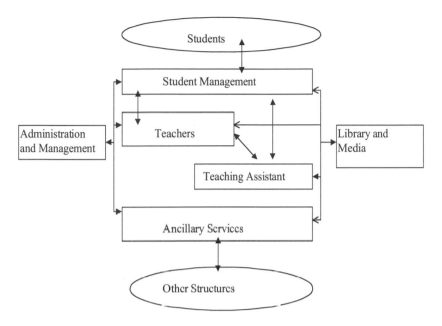

Figure 38: "Modular environment". This flow chart of a school information system is based on student information and focused on professional activities.

can be altered and re-prioritized. Options are available for making assignments to an entire class at once, copying assignments from one student to another and assigning either individual lessons or entire curricula. NovaNET automatically notifies instructors when students complete coursework or require new assignments. Summary statistics for the entire class are automatically captured.

A Common Architecture of Components

A consortium of academic, government, and commercial organizations called the IMS (for Instructional Management Systems) prepared a format for data that could be expected from an instructional management system so that other components of a university information system might work to that format (IMS, 2000). However, generally speaking *educational information systems architectures* have not been standardized. Health care information systems architectures have been standardized, and educational information systems have substantial overlap with health care information systems architectures. As the health care sector is ahead of the education sector in its use of information systems, progress in the health care area may inform the education arena.

The *Committee for European Normalization* has created standards for health care information system architectures (CEN, 2000). To modify these standards to address education, one can in some cases simply:

- replace "patient" with "student"

- replace terms for health care personnel or facilities with terms for related concepts about universities, teachers, libraries, and other education related personnel or facilities

Many interesting relationships exist between health care and education that might be further extended as the technological infrastructures for each are extended.

75

In any education organization, different types of actors perform activities, using resources and generating results. Activities may be either, directly or indirectly, related to the needs of students or to the general, managerial and organizational requirements of the organization. Depending on the type of activity, which is being executed, the results of one activity may represent education data of the students or, simply, other data to be communicated through the education organization. When executing one activity, a certain quantity of several resources is also used, such as staff members, computers, content, or libraries. The utilization of each resource has its specific cost, depending on the specific resource involved and on the type of activity performed. Different types of users are authorized to work with the education information system, and are allowed to perform various activities or access the different types of information.

Student information represents the central issue in the whole education information system. From the organizational and educational points of view, the *student component* is able to support the proper management, tracking and follow-up of the contacts had by the student with the education organization, either as resident, commuter, or distance student.

Resources are necessary for enabling the enterprise to work. Various types of resources may be identified, such as personnel (education, technical, administrative), materials including books, computers and even the individual locations where the work is performed. To support the needs of the various types of users properly, all applications need to take into account the characteristics and availability of the resources which are supposed to be used in each individual case.

The definition and control of the authorization of individual users in the execution of various activities and in the access to different information represents a major concern in the education environment. Two fundamental and complementary needs can be identified for the information system:

- the security of the managed data;

- the control and monitoring of the actual authorization for individual users executing certain activities on the system.

Security relates to the criteria and mechanisms according to which data must be managed, e.g. stored, transmitted and manipulated, by the overall system to ensure an adequate level of reliability and protection. Such aspects may also imply, amongst others, the enciphering of the information and the utilization of specific devices to ensure the correct identification of individuals. As a consequence, security represents a characteristic of the system closely dependent on and related to technological features.

- Apart from the need for ensuring the intrinsic security of the data, another major requirement can be identified in the need of the individual university to define criteria and rules according to which the individual users may be authorized to access the system and perform the various activities, according to their specific role and responsibility in the organization.

A name, a unique public identifier, and some mechanisms for ensuring its correct identification can characterize each user. To access a component, the agent must be a member of one authorization profile of that component. Such membership is granted by another individual user and is valid in a specific time period only.

A Structure/Function Model

The Education Information Systems Architecture has been viewed in terms of Education Components. In Figure 38 "Modular Environment" a *structural/functional view of an education information system* is presented. Students go through a student management module to teachers, administration, library, and other services. Teachers manage teaching assistants who in turn interact with students through the student management module and have access to library and ancillary services. The model does not address important concerns, such as marketing, finance, or course production.

The model addresses principally *the teaching function*:

- The course material is stored in the library as lessons. Lessons are grouped into courses, which are in turn linked into certificate and degree programs.

- Students have a record that identifies students and points to lesson accomplishments that are recorded separately for each student and each lesson.

- Teachers each have identification records too. Additionally, a record of transactions by the teacher with the student management and teaching assistants is maintained.

- Administration collects student evaluations of teacher performance and manages the assignment of teachers to courses and curricular management.

With such extensive recording of teaching-related activities, quality control of teaching is facilitated.

An indication of the breadth of possible *support services* in a university notes these four categories of such support (Lawrence and Service, 1977):

- Academic Support

- Student Service

- Institutional Support

- Student Access

Academic support is further decomposed into Computing, Course Development, and Academic Personnel Development. Student Service is basically counseling and depending on the student body may involve support for students to advance in their job. Institutional Support includes logistics, administrative computing, faculty services, and public relations. Student Access includes student recruitment and financial aid administration.

The *roles* in the university include student, teacher, librarian, administrator, marketer, budgeter, personnel manager, and course developer. The librarians acquire course material from third parties. The marketer develops relationships with future students and sells the course. The budgeter distributes revenue from student tuition fees to cost centers. Each role can be implemented in different ways but should have a well-specified interface that allows other roles to communicate with it.

Digital Nervous System

Bill Gates' book *Business @ the Speed of Thought* shares some themes with this book, which will be discussed in this section. To get a better flow of information, to develop the right processes and strategies, universities can take advantage of their information technology and create a digital nervous system.

Information work is thinking work. When thinking and collaboration are significantly assisted by computer technology, a digital nervous system exists. It consists of the advanced digital processes that knowledge workers use to make better decisions. To benefit from the digital age, universities can extend their digital infrastructure. Universities can improve their ability to run smoothly and efficiently, to respond to opportunities, to get valuable information to the people in the university who need it, and the ability to interact online with the various constituents of the university, including students, alumni, government, and industry.

A university's faculty and staff, not just its administrators, need to be aware of the activities of the university and to have access to rich information about students, other faculty, and the university. Ultimately, the most important "speed" issue for universities is cultural. It's changing the perceptions within a university about the rapidity with which everybody can move. Once the mind-set adapts to the need for action, digital technology enables fast reflexes.

Knowledge management is not a software product or a software category. Knowledge management starts with objectives and processes and recognition of the need to share information. Knowledge management is nothing more than managing information flow, and getting the right information to the people who need it so that they can act on it quickly.

The people in a university should collaborate effectively so that all of the key people on a project are well-informed and energized. The ultimate goal is to have a team develop the best ideas from throughout the university and then act with the same unity of purpose and focus that a single, well-motivated person would bring to bear on a situation. Digital information flow can support this group cohesiveness.

Quality control requires that an organization's activities are documented to be in line with its objectives. ISO 9000 is a quality control process standard, and a university can be certified as ISO 9000 compliant. Such certification could help a university convince students to enroll. Another approach to quality assurance is through government or professional societies that set standards for performance and certify a university or part of the university as conforming to the standard.

Reengineering principles combined with digital processes can lead to improvements. Creating a new process is a major project. To properly reengineer a process using technology requires the oversight of someone who can bridge the academic and technical teams. This academic process owner does not have to be the most senior or the most technical person on the academic side, but the person does have to understand the academic need and how the technology will be used in actual work. The person must be respected enough in the organization to make decisions stick.

The President should become as engaged in information technology, as in any other important academic function. The President needs a baseline understanding of technology. The President and Provost need to regard technology not as a cost but as a strategic resource for the academic side.

The university should measure information technology costs carefully, of course, but ultimately should judge its infrastructure in terms of the academic value it gives. A good infrastructure will cut baseline costs, but the leaders should always be asking what the infrastructure enables rather than what costs it reduces. Each year, the university should strive to spend a smaller percentage of resources on routine functions and a greater percentage on new solutions.

The university's information system should be based on educational information systems architecture. The architecture includes resources and activities and emphasizes modularity and interchangeability. Contemporary systems should provide Web interfaces that facilitate ready access to the organization from all of its constituents.

Figure 39: "Across Boundaries". This photo of flags from countries around the world is related to the theme that Web-enabled education can cross boundaries, including geopolitical boundaries.

New Marketing Opportunities

The reader should understand

- how the Web is expanding the marketing opportunities for universities,
- the importance of employee and customer education,
- some examples of online education by companies to their own employees, and
- how brokers and publishers can impact online education.

The Internet creates vast new opportunities for marketing (see Figure 39 "Across Boundaries"). In the first instance, universities are compelled to provide information about themselves to prospective students on the Web and to offer to interact with prospective students on the Internet. More significantly, the university might adopt strategies for teaching new groups of students not previously reached. Special relationships between the university and employers become possible through the Internet. Will universities want these opportunities? In addition to new opportunities to reach employees, universities face new competition from brokers and publishers who can connect teachers and students in ways not practical before the Web.

Figure 40: "New York Stock Exchange". This facade of the New York Stock Exchange is a symbol of corporate activity.

Using the Internet to Advertise

The Internet can be used to support advertising. Over ninety percent of college-bound students have Internet access and over half actively use email. High school juniors and seniors surf the Web as part of their college search and expect instant feedback. Prospective students who give institutions their email addresses often expect to get email (Magna, 2000).

A successful Web site at a university should build relationships, generate a sense of community, and engage interaction. Web sites should be database driven, allowing changes that used to require complicated technical manipulations to become simple clerical tasks. Sites should be dynamic, customizable, and interactive.

The university can use email to automatically respond to routine inquiries in a way that is immediate and tailored to inquirers' specific requests. If a Web visitor indicates an interest in, for example, on-campus housing, majoring in education, and basketball, an email can be sent automatically, thanking him or her for the interest and including prewritten items from the database covering the information requested. The email could also redirect the interested party to specific pages on the university Web site by including URLs — for example, "Please see the diagram showing the layout of our residence hall rooms by looking at www.yourschool.edu/housing.html."

Email direct marketing is also an effective way to call attention to special events that are either on the university campus or in a specific region. Email can be targeted and personalized by zip code or area code, academic interest, age/high school year, test scores, co-curricular interests, sports, and level of interest. Email direct marketing has the demonstrated ability to increase yield and to segment, personalize, and target messages while decreasing both response time to inquiry and cost per contact.

Educating Employees and Customers

In addition to offering new advertising options, the Web lifestyle changes the environment of education. Organizations can provide new patterns of education across space, time, and organizational boundaries. Will global businesses work with universities to educate employees and customers through the Web?

Global Giants

Large, globally distributed companies *institutionalize education* to successfully perpetuate their internal culture. Shareholders buy and sell stock in the company based on the company's ability to earn profits (see figure 40 "New York Stock Exchange"), but the ability to succeed in a business depends on customer and employee interest in the business. Education is one way for companies to positively influence employee and customer interest.

Xerox started the office copier business in 1959 and is now one of the world's largest corporations. The Education and Learning Division of Xerox is responsible for the policies and programs designed to educate Xerox employees. Xerox spends hundreds of millions of dollars each year on employee education. To quote from the Xerox Vice-President for Education and Learning (Xerox, 2000):

> Worldwide Xerox Education and Learning is leading the way as Xerox moves toward the virtual university. It is helping Xerox organizations around the world combine advanced learning techniques with new technologies to deliver training to the student, when and where it is needed.

Xerox wants to be a learning organization and believes that the most effective and productive employees are those who approach work itself as an opportunity for continuous learning.

GTE is a global telecommunications company with an interest in exploiting telecommunications to educate employees. The extract from a GTE employee email bulletin illustrates the intention of reaching people at their desktop with just in time, anytime education (GTE, 1997):

> GTE's Organizational Learning and Competency Development group is utilizing the intranet to offer new courses to all employees. Four separate education programs currently are being developed for delivery to employees through the intranet home page. The first program, the Balance Sheet, now is available ... these programs are engaging, interactive, involve no cost to employees and personally are efficient because they're available at employees' desktops. They are designed to help you become more knowledgeable on the financial aspects of our business, yet not require you to attend a formal classroom. Additionally, course descriptions, program schedules and on-line registration also can be accessed through the intranet home page.

Companies have long had education programs but with the rapidly changing business environment, the need for *employee education* has grown. Sometimes the employer wants the employee to have access to degree-based training and at other times to company-specific education. Additionally, companies may want to educate their customers. These trends are important to universities to understand in order to improve marketing of university education by establishing new relationships with employers (Teare et al. 1999).

Boeing has 15,000 engineers. Fewer than 2 percent are involved in graduate level engineering education programs. United Technologies is a company similar to The Boeing Company but sends 6 percent of its engineering population to part-time graduate education at various universities, and the United Technologies company goal is to increase that to 18 percent. Boeing intends to be more like United Technologies in its participation rate for engineers in graduate education. That means increasing its annual *enrollment* from a few hundred to a few thousand. At that point, The Boeing Company enrollment is comparable to that of a substantial higher education institution.

Boeing does not want to duplicate the efforts that universities already invest in creating and delivering educational programs. Accordingly, Boeing has put forward its requirements to the higher education community and is looking for partners to provide the education. Boeing wants its engineers to be able to earn a degree from a *university* but to be able to stay at the Boeing workplace. The student and teacher should be able to easily communicate across space and time. In the old model, Boeing gets videotapes recorded earlier, and a mentor on site works with students as they progress through the videotapes. In the new model, Boeing uses the Internet and other technologies to further support its education. In either case, Boeing pays full university tuition costs for its students.

In summary, large corporations institutionalize employee educational programs. Xerox puts every employee through educational programs. GTE has placed employee training programs on the intranet. The Boeing Company intends to have thousands of its engineers each year being educated on the job by universities using the information superhighway. This snapshot of some corporate activities would readily be extended to many other companies.

Industry Patterns

To improve one's understanding of the attributes of organizations that widely use the Web for educational purposes, one might study the content of the Web. *Content analysis* is a well-established method in social research that has been typically applied to paper document sources (e.g., Todd et al. 1995). The Web offers a new and rich source of information for content analysis.

Three very different *industry categories* were studied (Fortune, 2000) computer and data services, airline, and pipeline. At each of the company Web sites the company to its own employees performed a search for evidence of educational offerings. The *airline companies* provided more extensive evidence on the Web of a commitment to educating their own staff, than do the computer companies. This was most commonly of the form of education for pilots or flight attendants. In general, companies that have a large workforce, wide geographical distribution, and a need for training have the greatest evidence of Web educational activity.

Associate of Arts Degree in Telecommunications

The National Advisory Coalition for Telecommunications Education and Learning (NACTEL) was formed in 1997 to address education needs in the telecommunications industry (NACTEL, 2000). Funding from the Sloan Foundation enabled the development of a standardized associate's degree in telecommunications that is delivered through an online, asynchronous learning format. The degree is delivered to network technicians in the telecommunications industry.

The NACTEL members include four of the largest telecommunications companies in the United States (Bell Atlantic, GTE, SBC, and US West) and the two biggest unions representing network technicians (Communications Workers of America and International Brotherhood of Electrical Workers). Pace University delivers the Associate of Science Degree in Telecommunications. The NACTEL degree:

- is jointly sponsored by companies and unions,

- is a standardized credential that is recognized across the industry,

- offers Prior Learning Assessment options to students, and

- is available to students at any time and in any place.

The learning objectives were developed by NACTEL and the courses implemented by Pace University (Pace, 2000). The courses are instructor-led courses and utilize a variety of media, including Web, textbooks, videotapes, email, and online discussions. The seventeen courses in this degree include three electronics, four telecommunications, an English, a sociology, a business, and a few other courses. Furthermore, the education is recognized as comparable to two years of university education and credits are transferable to a bachelor's degree. The educational program began formal development for delivery in the fall of 1998 and opened to its first 100 students in the spring of 1999, increased enrollment to about 1000 students in the fall of 1999, and anticipates over ten thousand students to be enrolled each year in the twenty-first century.

Customers are Students

Novell Corporation develops computer network software. Some employers say that a new employee with a certificate from Novell earns more than a new employee with a masters degree in Business Administration. These *Novell certificates* are part of a broader mission of Novell to increase its market share (Novell, 2000):

> Novell Education's mission is to drive global pervasive computing through quality education programs and products; its purpose is to increase literacy on Novell products and technologies and thereby foster Novell's success worldwide. Novell Education plays a critical role in providing true pervasive computing by building the infrastructure of support and literacy that is necessary to drive and sustain that vision.

In other words, Novell is educating its customers so as to sell its networking products better. What is happening industry-wide as regards such education in virtual mode? One of the greatest markets for the growth of virtual education involves companies and their customers.

Oracle Corporation is the world's largest database management system company. Synergy exists between online education and Oracle's technology and education expertise (Oracle, 2000). Oracle has education centers in almost every country and hundreds of online educational offerings. Oracle University offers online, ongoing educational service for customers. Oracle University addresses the continuous, Web-based educational needs of modern organizations. People can earn a masters by completing all of the required courses in an Oracle Masters Program.

While competent employees are vital to success, so are satisfied customers, and virtual education has a special niche to fill as regards education of customers. State-funded educational organizations are not well prepared to compete with a global company that offers education specifically related to the company products. The developing marketplace is fast changing, and companies must look for opportunities to both differentiate themselves from their competitors and to insure long-term success – virtual education is one such attractive opportunity.

Brokers

This section will develop a classification of sole function brokers, show how teachers or students are represented by other organizations, study a self-organizing catalog of courses, and consider franchising of educational brokers. The sole function broker must be prudent to successfully compete with the other participants in the brokering business, such as publishers, who have primary revenue from other sources and can subsidize the educational aspects as a means of facilitating their primary business.

The Model

A *broker* (see Figure 41 "Broker") acts as an agent for others, as in negotiating contracts, purchases, or sales in return for a fee or commission (Merriam, 2000). A broker functions partly as a clearing house which exchanges checks and drafts and settles accounts. The broker in virtual education would not be a check clearinghouse but an education credits and fees clearinghouse.

How will content experts be able to enter information into a brokering system, and that system and expertise become accessible to those who need it to learn? A system would resemble a quick version of a *copyright clearance center*. The students purchase the copyrighted material in the end, although teachers and administrators will typically choose required content.

Teachers and administrators would offer courses at a certain fee for students and with a certain limit on enrollment in the courses. Teachers and administrators who had successfully marketed themselves would succeed and others not. Individual teacher performance statistics could be made available from continual quality control procedures. Students would thus know about the quality of the teacher before choosing to enroll in a particular class. Teachers would retain their traditional role as experts in the delivery of instruction, however classes would now be distributed across locales and time zones. Students would have more choice and the *teacher-marketplace* would be more competitive.

The broker connects students and teachers across space, time, and organizational boundaries. Teachers operate on an open market that encourages them to perform well in order to attract students. Brokering is easy to do in virtual mode over the Internet.

The sole function broker has no other function than to bring teachers and students together. As one considers the different methods of sole function brokers, one might devise a further decomposition *of sole function broker types*. Some connect schools to companies; some connect individual teachers to the public, and some provide an open catalog.

Figure 41: "Broker". The man in the middle has brokered a relationship between the man and woman shaking hands.

School ⇔ Company

Realizing that much of the teaching expertise is in schools in the form of full-time teachers, a brokering organization might seek to make alliances with schools for their teachers to participate in special educational programs. Likewise, realizing that companies may represent students with educational needs, a broker might seek contracts with companies for their students to be enrolled in courses. Thus occurs the *school ⇔ company broker*.

For higher education, the pre-eminent example of such a 'school ⇔ company' broker comes in the form of the *National Technological University* (NTU), based in the USA. NTU is a private, accredited, non-profit institution founded in 1984 to meet the advanced educational needs of working engineers, scientists and technical managers. NTU serves as a broker between universities and companies. Courses taught at a university are broadcast by satellite to receiving stations at certain, enrolled companies.

Figure 42: International University Home Page. The introductory links take one to degree offerings, courses, faculty, administration, and online registration.

More than one thousand courses are available through NTU, and a student can earn over a dozen master of science degrees. Primarily the faculty of about fifty engineering schools teaches these courses from some of the best universities in the United States (NTU, 2000). NTU engages in careful quality control procedures and will only allow teachers to participate in the program when they continually receive good student reports. The selection of *courses and teachers* is larger than a student would have at any one university.

To enroll in courses, students are typically employees of a company that is a member of the NTU Satellite Network. NTU has contracts with the companies, and the *companies provide the students*. About one thousand NTU sites exist across the United States. The companies involved include giants like General Motors, and their downlink sites can be anywhere in the world.

The NTU example has not been as exploited in the world by other organizations as it might. It takes advantage of the administrations already existing in schools and companies. By connecting sets of teaching organizations with sets of companies one reduces the *administrative overhead* for the broker. Thus the broker has a natural advantage in offering a large amount of education to the workplace in virtual mode.

In summary, the school ⇔ company broker arranges contracts whereby schools provide teachers and companies provide students. The National Technological University is a prime example of such a broker. Companies make contracts with NTU for their employees to get NTU education from teachers around the world. Other educational organizations are adopting this broker mode of operation.

Teacher ⇔ Student

At the other extreme from the NTU model of making alliances with schools and companies for their teachers and students, respectively, are organizations that only make individual contracts with students and with teachers. Many organizations exist that connect teachers to students by advertising publicly for teachers and students. Anyone is welcome to come forward individually as a possible teacher or student. Examples of such *teacher* ⬄ *student* virtual educational organizations include the Jones International University, the International School for Information Management University, and the Western Governors University.

Jones International University

The *Jones International University* serves the Internet community (see Figure 42 "International University"). Teaching contracts are with individual teachers from universities who form a virtual faculty of Jones International University. The faculty work full-time at other universities and work on short-term, part-time contracts for the International University. Students are recruited from the general public.

The International University degrees include a Master of Arts in Business Communication and a Bachelor of Arts Completion Degree in Business Communications (JIU, 2000). The *curriculum* combines the fields of Human Communication and New Communications Technologies. Examples of courses include one on Communications Ethics and another on Using the Internet in Business. Thirty-five credit hours must be completed to earn the masters degree, and a bachelors degree requires 120 credit hours

Students can visit samples of the courses online without registering to decide whether or not the course and method are for them. Students *apply online* for admission to the B.A. or M.A degree program. Upon admission into the B.A or M.A. program, students work with an advisor to establish a Degree Plan that is tailored to meet the student's individual learning needs. Students also enroll in individual courses on-line. The student pays approximately $200 per credit hour.

International School of Information Management

Another example of a teacher ⬄ student virtual educational organization is the *International School of Information Management* (ISIM). ISIM is similar to the International University that was started in 1987 (Boehm, 2000).

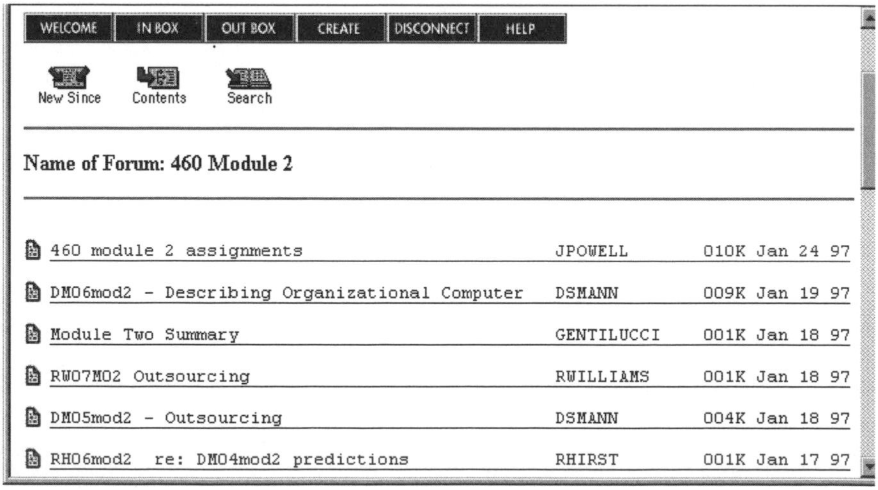

Figure 43: ISIM Interface. This is a portion of the screen as the student sees it, while taking a course. The top icons give access to the email in box and out box and other opportunities. The rows in the lower half of the screen link to a teacher or student. submission.

ISIM has a *faculty* of experts around the world. ISIM faculty includes university professors, business executives, and consultants. As for the International University, faculty has full-time employment elsewhere than ISIM. ISIM has 100 students enrolled in its graduate degree program and 250 students taking various individual executive courses. ISIM actively recruits *students* from the general public via advertisements in trade journals and elsewhere

ISIM is *accredited* through the Distance Education and Training Council, which is in turn recognized as the sole accrediter for distance education by the United States Department of Education. Students pay $375 per credit hour and a course is typically 3 credit hours. A masters degree requires 36 credits but 40 percent of these may be transferred into the program. Students work at their own pace and graduate whenever they finish the requirements.

Through ISIM one may study online interactive programs (electronic classrooms) or guided self-study programs (print-based materials). The standard online offerings at ISIM are based on essentially *email news group*s. The teacher posts readings and assignments via email and students ask questions and submit exercise answers via email. The Internet infrastructure for ISIM is a kind of bulletin board that has been tailored for ISIM's educational purposes (see Figure 43 "ISIM Interface"). Students may read assignments submitted online by the teacher. They submit exercise answers or questions via electronic bulletin board. The teacher or student can search or browse the archive.

Western Governors University

Government is typically involved in education by collecting taxes that subsidize general education in the state. This is already one kind of broker role. However, a new kind of phenomenon is due to technology and the opportunities for virtual education. Some of the Western Governors of the United States formed an alliance to facilitate the development of a virtual university that operates as a broker of education. What was done by the western states of the United States is also being done by other groups of *states*.

The plans for the *Western Governors University* (WGU) began in 1995. The governors wanted to expand educational opportunities by offering courses from a wide array of sources and reaching a wide array of students. The particular focus is on reaching students at the workplace with teachers coming from various existing educational organizations (WGU, 2000).

The WGU is a nonprofit, independent corporation with a board of trustees composed of the governors from each participating state. The WGU is

- *market-oriented*, paying particular attention to developing education markets and needs and

- *competency-based*, certifying learning and competency, not seat time.

Both faculty and industry develop standards of quality for courses experts. These are used by a Regional Review Council to screen courses and programs that are candidates for listing in the WGU catalog.

The central operation is responsible for governance and policy, creates and maintains the WGU's key assets (the catalog and management systems), and does quality control. A pilot of the WGU catalog became operational in 1997. Educational organizations have submitted course descriptions to the WGU for inclusion in the catalog. In 1998, the WGU began marketing courses for institutions whose courses qualify for inclusion in the WGU *catalog*.

In 1999, WGU offered four degrees: a Master of Arts in Learning and Technology and three Associate of Arts Degrees. One Associates degree is a general subject one and the other two are computer network administration and electronic manufacturing. Providers make offerings

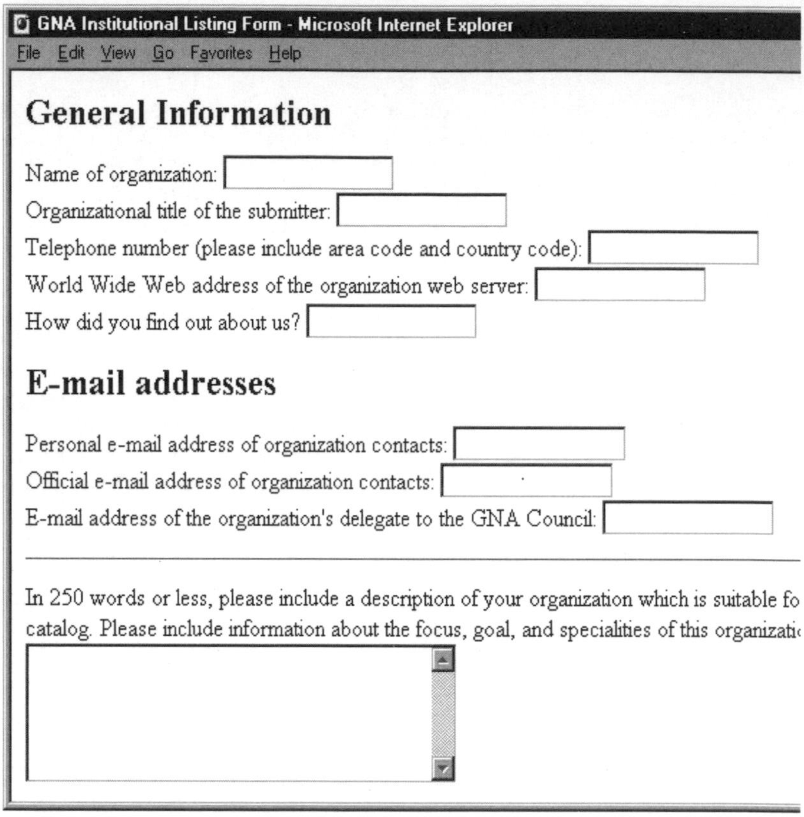

GNA Institutional Listing Form - Microsoft Internet Explorer

File Edit View Go Favorites Help

General Information

Name of organization: [   ]

Organizational title of the submitter: [   ]

Telephone number (please include area code and country code): [   ]

World Wide Web address of the organization web server: [   ]

How did you find out about us? [   ]

E-mail addresses

Personal e-mail address of organization contacts: [   ]

Official e-mail address of organization contacts: [   ]

E-mail address of the organization's delegate to the GNA Council: [   ]

In 250 words or less, please include a description of your organization which is suitable fo
catalog. Please include information about the focus, goal, and specialities of this organizatic

[   ]

Figure 44: "GNA Entry Form". The educator enters a description of course offerings into the GNA database through this form.

available through the technologies of their choice, and students choose courses based on the technologies they prefer or to which they have access.

Within the confines of the Western States of the United States, the Western Governors University faces *competition* of various sorts. For instance, the most populous state represented in the Western Governors Association, namely California, decided that it would rather develop its own virtual university than is part of an effort led by other western states. After a few years, however, California abandoned its own California Virtual University but still did not elect to join the Western Governors University.

More generally, some educational institutions within the political boundaries of WGU are cautious about the WGU and concerned about the impact of the WGU on traditional programs. There is tension on these campuses over faculty compensation and tenure for faculty who invest time and intellectual energy on distance education. Community colleges and four-year colleges and universities with strong adult education programs have been most involved. Faculty at universities with a research orientation is sometimes opposed to the WGU because, in part, they fear a reduction in time for research when distance education is emphasized.

Catalogs and Auctions

The most basic broker provides a catalog of courses. For distance education courses an online catalog is particularly relevant. Providers of traditional paper catalogs for traditional universities and their courses are now providing online catalogs and providing portals for distance education customers. For instance, Peterson's which has catalog university courses since 1966, started in 1995 to provide online access to a directory of distance education courses (Peterson, 2000). Multiple new entrants to this catalog market have appeared such as newpromise.com, which started in 1999, and claims to be (newpromise, 2000) "the most complete source of online courses and degrees from fully accredited colleges and universities nationwide."The Directors and Advisors of newpromise.com are famous professors from Harvard University and Massachusetts Institute of Technology.

The *Globewide Network Academy* (GNA) was one of the first organizations to provide an online catalog of distance education courses. GNA created in 1993 a program on the World Wide Web that solicits others to enter information about distance education courses. Educational organizations can enter descriptions of courses that can be taken at a distance. Students can browse the database to find courses that they might want to take.

The operation of GNA is basically automatic. Institutions or individuals go to forms at the GNA site and enter descriptions of their offerings including pointers to Web sites (see Figure 44 "GNA Entry Form"). In addition to the questions indicated in the figure, the form collects information about the accreditation status of the institution, the details of the courses being offered, and registration information. In this way, a student who wants to take a course that has been identified on GNA, can go directly from the GNA site to the site where registration for the course is handled or, at least, instructions are given as to how one might register. Another forms interface allows institutions to modify their own course descriptions anytime. The GNA Web catalog (GNA, 2000) describes over 9000 courses and 500 degree programs from 400 institutions.

The catalog that is created by these submissions from institutions and individuals is the product offered to students. The catalog is *searchable and browsable*. The user can find listings of hundreds of courses that are offered in distance education mode in a wide range of disciplines from around the world. On identifying relevant instructional offerings, the student is then expected to contact the teaching organization directly, as GNA does not itself register students or engage in the actual delivery of education.

Many organizations can create a Web site and invite others to enter information into it. However, once created, someone must also regularly *maintain* the Web server. The institutions and public that visit the site must find something special there.

One way to give such a catalog additional functionality would be to add an auction facility. For instance, Georgetown University, USA, invited students to apply for positions in a course through an online auction. In the auction format, Georgetown University officials set a $10,000 starting price as well as an undisclosed minimum price that they were willing to accept in the auction (Carr, 2000). The Web site's computer continually reduced the asking price for places in the Georgetown course, so that all seats in it eventually filled, even if at prices lower than Georgetown originally sought (see Figure 45 "Web Auction for Course"). A buyer could purchase a seat in the course at the current price calculated by the computer, or the buyer could place a sealed bid that is lower than the current price. If the price dropped to the point where it reached a sealed bid without the seat's going to a higher bidder, the bidder would win the seat at that price.

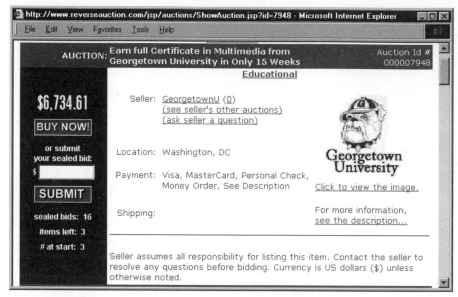

Figure 45: "Web Auction for Course". This Web site (ReverseAuction, 2000) is offering students an opportunity to enroll in a course with tuition based on the auction method. The current going price is indicated in the left-hand side of the figure and continuously declines until enough bids have been received to fill the course.

Such auctions can be done at any Web auction site. The most successful Web auction site in terms of gross volume is eBay. However, specialist auction sites may be appropriate for specialist services, such as higher education. One natural site to extend its services to include auction features is an online catalog of distance education courses.

Franchises and Consultants

Essentially every business model can be applied to the education market. Under the broad interpretation of brokers might also be included franchises. A *franchise* is a type of business in which a group or individual receives a license to conduct a commercial enterprise. Franchises enable a franchisee to market a well-known product or service in return for an initial fee and a percentage of gross receipts. The franchiser usually provides assistance with merchandising and advertising and is a kind of broker.

One example of a franchise operation that supports education is *The Fourth R* – its sole function is education and computers are both the subject and the tool. The term Fourth R refers to the four Rs of reading, writing, arithmetic, and information technology (Fourth, 2000). A Fourth R Authorized Education Center provides:

- a plan that matches school resources with technology objectives,
- step by step activities and projects that can be integrated with current classroom objectives, and
- initial start-up and software specific training for school staff.

The Fourth R goal is to help schools to help students take advantage of the computer as a tool for research, homework, and communication.

How does a franchise operate financially? An organization that wants to become a franchise of The Fourth R needs to initially pay The Fourth R an initiation fee of about $20,000 (Park, 1997). Once in operation the franchisee pays The Fourth R a monthly royalty fee of 5 percent for all sales plus a flat fee of $100 per month. In exchange for these *fees* the franchisee gets support in being an Authorized Education Center of The Fourth R. These franchisee financial arrangements are similar to what they might be in non-education businesses.

Publishers

Publishers in the education marketplace have long served a kind of broker role. They contract with expert authors to produce books or other products that they feel students will want to buy. *Publishers* also often work between the author of content and the teacher who will deliver the content. In any case, the publisher is fundamentally a broker in education. The growth of the Internet and particularly the Web has threatened the traditional revenue stream of some publishers, and most are exploring various ways to work on the information superhighway. One approach is to offer education that uses the materials of the publisher. The cases of McGraw-Hill and Ziff Davis as publishers in online education are presented next.

A Diverse Conglomerate

Founded in 1888, the McGraw-Hill Companies provide information and analysis in multiple media. Sales in 1996 were over $3 billion. Two of the many divisions of *McGraw-Hill* that were involved in virtual education were *National Radio Institute* (NRI) and the Continuing Education Division in the USA. NRI had permanent teaching staff and was thus not a true broker in the sense used in this chapter but had important brokering characteristics. The Continuing Education Division was a broker in the strict sense.

In 1914 a high school teacher started giving extra instruction to four of his students in the new field called "wireless radio." This teacher next turned his part-time efforts into a full-time career, and the NRI was born. In 1966 McGraw-Hill purchased NRI.

NRI offered high-tech electronics, computer-based, and occupational education programs. NRI was an accredited member of the *Distance Education and Training Council*. For many years NRI enrolled over 38,000 students annually.

NRI claims (NRI, 2000) to be the first organization to:

• educate students on a digital computer with training software or

• use multimedia computers and the Web to familiarize students with cutting-edge technology.

NRI utilized technical publishing resources of The McGraw-Hill Companies. However, NRI also invested about $3 million annually in *course development*. Its 200 staff included development engineers, writers, editors, illustrators, instructors, and technical support personnel. However, in 2000 McGraw-Hill decided that the business opportunities for NRI had changed and that it reorganized its online education offerings.

The McGraw-Hill Online Learning unit (McGraw-Hill, 2000) supports continuing education for professionals. One component addresses Certified Public Accountants (CPAs). CPAs need to engage in life-long continuing education in order to remain certified. The McGraw-Hill online and self-study courses allow CPAs to fulfill their Continuing Professional Education credit requirements over the Internet (McGraw-Hill, 2000). The CPA gets study guides, takes examinations, and earns credits over the Internet. Experts throughout the USA write McGraw-Hill CPA courses. These experts are either practicing accounting somewhere or working for a higher education institution, in addition to authoring material for McGraw-Hill.

Specialty Publisher

Ziff Davis is a specialist publishing company. It publishes books and magazines about popular computing subjects. In 1995 Ziff Davis extended its offerings by creating the ZD Net University. Courses at ZD Net University were typically based on material published by Ziff Davis and taught in part by the authors of the published material.

ZD Net University (ZDU) offered online computing classes and seminars taught on private, moderated *message boards*. Once a week, a qualified ZDU instructor posted an assignment on the class message board. The instructor, teaching assistants, moderators and other students, managed all discussion resulting from the assignment. Further details about the operation of a course included:

- Students logged onto ZDU at least once a week to read assignments and post questions.

- Most classes lasted 4 to 8 weeks.

- Instructors offered bi-weekly live chat 'office hours' for real-time interaction.

Typical Web browsers could view the message board classrooms (see Figure 46 "ZDU Classroom").

ZDU classes often required the student to purchase literature published by Ziff Davis. Thus these courses served as a kind of marketing arm for the core Ziff Davis product. The *tuition fees* that ZDU charged were very low and did not cover the full cost of creating and running a virtual

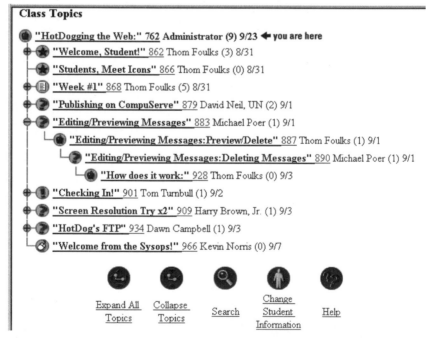

Figure 46: "ZDU Classroom". This online discussion system shows the topic of a participants contributions, the name of the contributor, and the date. The descendant relationship in the hierarchy is automatically created as one person replies to another person's contribution. Most of the discussion comes from students in the course and some from the teacher and teaching assistants.

university. Students paid no more than $5 a month to be enrolled in as many ZDU courses as they could enter. Students could earn Continuing Education Units from the American Board of Education when they completed a ZDU class online (for an additional processing fee).

In 1999 Ziff Davis bought SmartPlanet and moved ZDU to SmartPlanet (SmartPlanet, 2000). By 1999 ZDU had developed a customer base of 100,000 people. ZDU wanted to expand its operations further and thus the move to SmartPlanet. SmartPlanet maintains the courses and most of the policies of ZDU for the courses that ZDU had, but SmartPlanet also offers another range of courses and services.

Conclusion

University education has long been concerned to provide employers with graduates who would fit the needs of the employers. The opportunities of technology-enhanced education create further opportunities to connect universities with their employer constituents. Large companies, like Boeing and General Electric, are particularly notable for their employee markets. A company like Boeing has one quarter of a million employees and in encouraging engineers to get a graduate education provides more student engineers than a single university can comfortably accommodate.

While information technology topics are the ones often first suitable to the Internet as a mode of delivery, other industries, such as the airline industry, are also in need of continuing education. An example of an education targeting the employees of a company or companies is the Associate of Telecommunications. The big American telecommunications companies and labor unions have sponsored that online degree and are fundamental to the associates degree being a success.

While employers can be key contacts for a university in offering online education to employers, the employers might prove in the long run to be a yet more vital contact for reaching the customers of the employer. Consider for example a market research company that wants to help its customers understand its market research results. For some of the customers a formal education related to topics of market research might be particularly helpful and be important to the market research company, its customers, and the universities.

Brokers try to put together those organizations or individuals that have education needs and those organizations or individuals that provide education to external audiences. Brokers typically do not have their own staff of educators nor any particular monopoly on an audience to receive education. In virtual mode, these brokers wish to offer

- certain teachers on the Internet the opportunity to have a greater audience and

- certain students on the Internet an opportunity for an education.

For instance a teacher in Germany offers a course in computer languages via a broker in the USA. A student in Korea takes the course on the Internet via the broker.

The sole function education broker has no function other than to broker education. By contrast, a publisher that creates opportunities for authors of its textbooks to teach on the Internet is not primarily a broker but is primarily a publisher. A *sole function broker* may itself take many forms of which three categories are "between university and company", "between teacher and public", and "open catalog":

- The National Technological University helps connect universities to companies. It has been in the business for many years and has dozens of universities and companies in its regular stable of clients.

- Various organizations recruit excellent teachers from universities or other organizations and put together a curriculum to which are then recruited students from the public or from companies – the Jones International University and International School of Information Management fits in this category.

- The "open catalog" broker may simply provide a Web site as a catalog into which teachers or schools can enter descriptions of distance education courses and students can search to find courses that suit their educational needs. The Globewide Network Academy invites anyone to describe an online course offering and anyone to search the database that has resulted from these entries.

Brokers have the advantage of flexibility, as they do not make fixed, lifetime appointments to their teachers.

Publishers are natural for-profit organizations to move into the virtual education broker business. Publishers have been brokers for centuries. Within the educational sector their job has been to find teachers to write textbooks and then to persuade other teachers to order the book for their classes. In certain cases, this is a short distance from finding teachers to offer courses and students to take the courses. Furthermore, the publisher can gain further exposure for its own publications by using them in the virtual courses that it brokers.

McGraw-Hill is one of the largest publishing companies in the world and has several subdivisions that are engaged in education. In its Certified Public Accountant educational program teachers from various organizations are aligned with students. Publications from McGraw-Hill are used in its virtual educational activities.

The *Ziff Davis* publishing organization has a most unusual pricing structure for its virtual university. Its virtual university charges students less than $5 per month for unlimited enrollment in courses that last about a month each. Ziff Davis can thus sell more of its publications because those publications are used in its courses.

The *marketplace* is changing rapidly. Many alliances are possible between universities and companies, between universities and brokers, between universities and publishers, and among universities. The conditions under which one alliance will succeed and another will fail are complex functions of market strategy, leadership, and ability to work together.

Figure 47: "Universities @ Speed of Thought". The scholar's cap on the globe symbolizes higher education. The globe on the computer with a mailbox flag suggests a Web-enabled university.

Conclusion

Education perpetuates a culture. Information technology supports this education through:

- courseware for learning tasks;
- classrooms across time, space, and organizational boundaries; and
- universities that connect students and teachers across courses.

As the culture becomes progressively more Internet-oriented, universities have an obligation to understand what the Internet can do.

Summary

Education's cultural bias can be religious, political, economic, scientific, social, or otherwise. The evolution of technologies for dealing with knowledge is linked to education. Technological advances of the past half-century allow for large document collections and individual documents to be electronically manipulated over arbitrary distances. People can communicate over computer networks in multiple media. Through the continuing evolution of education and technology, culture will be perpetuated in increasingly sophisticated and diverse forms.

Education is achieved through learning. Learning is, in turn, achieved through the modification of a model in the student's mind. Rote memorization is a crude learning task, while synthetic reasoning accomplishes more sophisticated learning. Through *courseware* the computer supports learning tasks. At its simplest, courseware supports multiple-choice questions with instant feedback. An intelligent tutoring system uses domain, pedagogy, and student models in ways that human teachers do. These models can also help guide rich multimedia interactions in the form of virtual realities. However, the cost of building intelligent, virtual reality tutoring systems is currently prohibitively high for most occasions.

The production of sophisticated courseware may require specialist teams. This is not for the lone teacher to do, as is too often the case in universities. Different, highly specialized roles keep a precise schedule and produce sequentially linked deliverables in the courseware life cycle. People involved in *courseware production* require substantial organizational support.

Courseware may be used by a lone student or in the context of a classroom. In classroom learning the student interacts with other students and the teacher in order to gain further insights.

The *virtual classroom* exists on the information superhighway. Groupware technologies are particularly appropriate to the classroom. Groupware supports the activities of a group in synchronous or asynchronous mode. The simplest way to do this is to provide for online submission of exercise answers and electronic bulletin boards for discussion of those answers. Students may use a paper book for the core reading material. Groupware may be used for courses that still have regular face-to-face meetings, or all meetings might occur via the groupware and none in face-to-face mode. In the Studio Course, groupware complements lectures and courseware. The Studio Course has been shown to reduce the cost of traditional teaching and to improve quality. The virtual classroom allows teachers to manage the submission of work and student-student interactions in ways that would be impractical without the computer support.

A classroom exists within a university. The *virtual university* is a type of virtual organization. In a successful virtual organization, the technology fits into the workflow of the people. To place a university onto the information superhighway, one needs a model of the university. This model must accommodate students, teachers, administrators, marketers, and more. Information systems are commercially available which implement a simple model of a university and which can be tailored to a particular university's needs. One of the impediments to progress in this arena is the high cost of tailoring an information system to a particular university. Standards for universities and their information systems reduce the costs of individual university information systems. Standards for operation also facilitate quality control. Furthermore, with computer networks one can monitor many of the transactions within a university and automatically give feedback about the quality of performance of individuals within the university.

Education brokers link students and teachers. Sole function brokers have no other purpose than to broker education and gain their strength by their extensive reach into the market of teachers and students. Publishers are another kind of broker that traditionally focuses on the relationship between authors of content and teachers who recommend the material to their students. However, these publishers can take advantage of the information superhighway and become brokers that connect authors to students.

At every level of the educational enterprise – student, teacher, administrator, and society – the models of what happens need to be clear in order that the computer can be asked to help. Furthermore, as the computer assumes an assistant role at one level, people will become more aware of how important the interactions across levels are. People take these interactions for granted and deal with them instinctively after years of practice. However, computers must be told precisely what the teacher needs to know from the administrator, the administrator from society, and so on.

Five-year Future

Even in the medium term of five years, people have not proven adept at predicting what specific forms of technological support will be the most cost-effective, or even in common use, within higher education. For instance, in 1990 there was little inkling that use of the Internet would have the impact on higher education that it has had. Conversely, ten years ago, the use of artificial intelligence techniques was widely predicted to impact education and training but did not. However, general trends can be *predicted*.

The use of information technology will increase. This will correspond with an increasing access to appropriate facilities. Activities routinely in need of support will include:

- individual learning from courseware,
- local and distance communication, and
- access to remote resources.

The use of the *Internet* to support the latter of these two is expected to show particularly dramatic gains over the coming years.

Currently the principal strategies for teaching and learning in higher education are based on the spoken *lecture*. Although the lecture may be viewed as a cost-efficient means for transferring knowledge, in many lectures little student learning occurs and passive rather than active learning strategies are reinforced. Current educational approaches favor focused and purposeful problem-based learning, and appropriate use of dialogue among learners. This includes the ability to reason and seek creative solutions individually and in groups. Such interactive learning could increase over the coming years and be supported by Internet tools.

The *management* of classrooms, universities, and entire educational systems can be facilitated by information technology. By tracking each transaction between a student and the educational system, the computer can facilitate the decomposition of the educational enterprise in ways that give new options to the student and reduce costs. This process is occurring in numerous other enterprises, such as financial, manufacturing, and retail enterprises. Universities will continue over the next 5 years to adopt information technology but with neither the speed nor the effectiveness of some private enterprises.

What students will have the most to gain from virtual education over the next five years? Imbalances in demands for skills and the needs for life-long learning mean that *graduate retraining* is a growth area. Education offered over the Web is likely to be effective for graduates who are well-motivated and comfortable with the Web. This education would arrive at the workplace or home and be suited to the career advancement of the student. Companies will play increasing roles in sponsoring such education.

The uses to which information technology might be put over the next five years in education are many and varied. One principle will surely apply: when the technology *fits smoothly into the life style* of the intended users, then success is likely, and otherwise not. For instance, if the target audience has no computers but has to go to special facilities to use them, then some of the advantages of virtual education may be diminished. Likewise for teachers and administrators, if routine computer use is awkward, then the opportunities to use the technology are limited.

In summary:

- Changes in technology used by education have proven difficult to predict. However, the next five years should see a continued increase in the use of networked computing, such as via the Internet or its World Wide Web application. Lectures are no longer considered a quality method of educating, and interactive learning with the support of *computer networks* could become more common.

- The *management* of educational enterprises could benefit enormously from tracking extensively the transactions of its business. However, the lack of direct financial incentives for such improvement will militate against the kinds of improvements that one can witness in some businesses.

- Students in continuing education should become an increasingly large part of the total student population and be particularly suited to education delivered at the workplace or home. As the tools must be comfortable to the students who will use them, *high technology, continuing education students* will be prime targets initially for virtual education delivered via high technology.

While the rapid pace of change makes precise predictions even a few months in advance impossible, the aforementioned three, broad categories of trends seem secure.

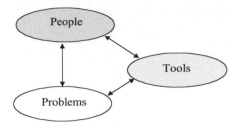

Figure 48: "People, Tools, Problems".

Thirty-year Future

Some experts say higher education is in crisis. Renowned management consultant and author Peter Drucker says (Lenzner and Johnson, 1997):

> Thirty years from now the big university campuses will be relics...It's as large a change as when we first got the printed book. Do you realize that the cost of higher education has risen as fast as the cost of health care?...Such totally uncontrollable expenditures, without any visible improvement in either the content or the quality of education, means that the system is rapidly becoming untenable.

However, Massy and Zemsky (1995) have said: "One must remember not to *confuse 'contact' with 'contact hours.'*" Some students will continue to want a traditional collegiate education with all its socialization (or contact), while others will just want the certification (or contact hours). Information technology will allow this separation and – moreover – allow a learner to choose either or both.

While the automation of universities systems was seen as unlikely in the five-year forecast, the educational organization will have become in thirty years more *effective and efficient* through the proper use of information technology. The judicious use of technology under inspired leadership can help a university separate content production from delivery, which can, in turn, be separated from assessment. Students, teachers, and administrators will better share information in ways that improve quality control.

The detailed shape of information technology thirty years hence is *difficult to predict*. Wireless computers the size of a credit card will receive data or multimedia information anywhere and anytime for some people. Artificial intelligence techniques will allow some roles in the organization to be performed by computers. To the extent that these or very different technologies become prevalent, they will be implemented first in non-educational organizations. For instance, the financial sector will use multimedia information and artificial intelligence before the education sector does. Nevertheless, in thirty years time some educational organizations should be significantly different from those today, while some will be little changed from their current situation.

New education marketplaces will rise in prominence over the next thirty years. More and more organizations will need to educate customers in order to keep their customers. State funded organizations have rather well-defined audiences and boundaries that often limit their ambitions as regards reaching new markets of students. In certain markets virtual education is already occurring between companies and customers. If political boundaries remain as crustacean as they have for millennia but the globalization of business continues, then corporate education may play an increasingly prominent role.

Dialectics

Dialectics is a practice of arriving at the truth by the exchange of logical arguments. In particular the practice is associated with the Marxian process of change through the conflicting of opposing forces, whereby a primary and a secondary aspect characterize a given contradiction. The secondary aspect succumbs to the primary but is then transformed into an aspect of a new contradiction.

Consider the mapping among *tools, problems, and people* from a dialectical perspective (see Figure 48 "People, Tools, and Problems"). If a certain tool supports technology-enhanced education, then for certain people with certain educational needs a certain tool can help. For other people or other educational needs the tool may well be inappropriate.

Now consider *changes across time*. For instance, a new tool appears. This new tool may be better for some combination of people and problems than the tool that they currently use. A tension exists between the established way of working and the new way that uses the new tool. For these people to resolve this tension, they may move to the new way of working. This move could occur gracefully and peacefully but sometimes the change may be awkward and conflict-laden. After the change, a peace prevails only so long as developments in people, their educational needs, or their tools do not require another transition in the way of work.

Consider the traditional classroom lecture for a fully employed adult who wants to earn a Master's Degree in Business Administration. Now the tool of the Web creates opportunities for students to earn their degree in virtual mode. As some students and teachers move to this form of study, they experience the tension of adapting to new ways. Examples for other tools, other students, and other courses of study are endless and through time new *combinations arise*.

The educational system has evolved rather slowly over the centuries, but will the pace of change quicken? To understand the directions that will be followed, one needs to understand the mapping among people, their tools, and their problems and how this mapping will change over time. Consider next some of the dominant *themes* that help explain how the maps are redrawn.

For people to take advantage of the power of the computer to help manage the *transactions* of education, the information about a transaction must be known by the computer. To this end, any activity involving non-computer media for which records should be maintained and monitored should also be encoded and entered into the appropriate computer storage. One theme of change will be the continued move of information into computers and the monitoring of student and teacher transactions through the computer networks.

Publishers are offering educational, multimedia, interactive CD-ROMs from which students can learn. The student can use these products at home, work, or university. The increasing presence of these tools will drive students to adjustments in the mapping of students and tools.

Friction-Free Education

Massy and Zemsky (1995) have said: "Information technology's strongest potential influence is that it will place the advantage with the learner rather than the institution, by creating a more effective market in learning, as opposed to a controlled allocation of scarce teaching resources." In his book *The Road Ahead* Bill Gates (see Figure "Gates") emphasizes the role of *friction-free capitalism* in the information age. When Adam Smith described the concept of markets in *The Wealth of Nations* in 1776, he theorized that if every buyer knew every seller's price, and every seller knew what every buyer was willing to pay, everyone in the market would be able to make fully informed decisions and society's resources would be distributed efficiently. To date we have not achieved Smith's ideal because would-be buyers and would-be sellers seldom have

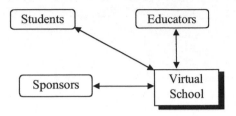

Figure 49: "Students, Educators, Sponsors".

complete information about one another. The information highway may extend the electronic marketplace and make it the universal middleman (Gates, 1996). For this low-friction, low-overhead scenario to attain market information must be plentiful and transaction costs low.

The application of friction-free capitalism to education means that the only humans involved in a transaction will be the actual *student and teacher* – with students and teachers from anywhere in the world able to connect. Why should students be restricted to enrolling in one institution and taking a course from that institution when there is another version of the course elsewhere that better suits them? If a student simply wants a course, why bother to have a university and not just let the student contact the teacher?

The *university* goes beyond the teacher-student relationship to certify a curriculum. A university structures a particular sequence of offerings and certifies it. In the open market of the information superhighway, the universities may continually reassess how their certificates compare with those of other universities. This tension to compete globally may drive the adoption of new tools for managing universities.

Education involves, at least, the *roles of student and teacher* (see Figure 49 "Students, Educators, Sponsors"). Beyond those basic roles, other roles include those of administrator and sponsor. Sponsors provide resources. The state is a major sponsor. Companies can also sponsor education either for employees or customers.

Sponsors that have a *captive audience* include the organization with an educational program for its employees or that can teach about its product to a customer who has no other credible source of education about the product (see Figure 50 "Captive Students"). The role of state universities creates a different kind of captivity. Students who go to state universities in their region get the benefit of reduced costs for themselves. A somewhat different kind of competitive factor occurs when an educational organization has permanent teaching staff—this is an aspect of being captive that is quite different from having a captive student but is also relevant to an understanding of the evolving geography of university education.

In some scenarios friction-free education is excellent. However, the socialist view might argue for a different approach. Does friction-free education collide with universal education? For education from childhood till death, records would document each student's educational past and

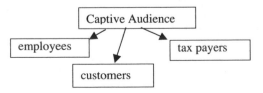

Figure 50: "Captive Students".

100

facilitate the seamless tailoring of further education to the student's particular needs and background. This tension between allowing people to freely connect on the one hand, and institutionalizing the support for their connections is a tension in the traditional *Marxist* sense of a dialectic (see Figure "Marx"). In what educational system will:

1) people be free to learn but

2) the records of students and teachers be managed by universities.

Friction-free education may be good for some students. For other students, managed education is more appropriate.

Some working people need further education in our rapidly changing digital world. *Global companies* with captive audiences of employees and customers may increasingly compete with one another through their sponsorship of virtual education. Global companies have boundaries that go beyond those of any particular government and have needs to perpetuate their own culture. This education may go beyond narrow training and may encompass combinations of theory and practice that will be relevant to the day-to-day experiences of the students. To these ends such companies should collaborate with existing higher education institutions to better prepare the company's employees and customers to deal with the kinds of products and services that the company produces.

Figure 51: Gates.

Epilogue

Individual students learning from courseware will have progressively more chances to experience teacher-like qualities in interaction with the computer. For now this kind of interactivity is basically in the form of multiple-choice questions and answers. However, the systems supporting such multiple-choice questions are being progressively extended to capture more knowledge of pedagogy, the domain, and the student and becoming more like intelligent, virtual reality tutoring systems.

Virtual classrooms have attracted the attention of many but often support no more interaction than email dialog. This situation will change, as the ways to manage student-student interactions online are better understood. In particular, the opportunities to have the teacher sample transactions between students and to give feedback so as to guide quality offer many new possibilities.

For the administration of the university the challenge is to get the organization to be precise about its objectives and ways of working and to take advantage of the digital nervous system. Ultimately, advances with courseware and virtual classrooms are stymied unless they can tap into the rich information that comes from the history of the student and her education that only the university can manage.

As the university reaches to new markets online, the role of employers, brokers, publishers, and other organizations in the society becomes more pronounced for the university. For instance, an employer with one-quarter million employees and with educational needs that are very pronounced and distinct may deserve special attention from a university or consortium of universities. The supervisors of particular employees may serve as mentors of those employees when they function as students in a part-time degree program. These connections between the academy and the outside world are being made precise and supported online.

The models under which students, teachers, administrators, and society operate must be clear before the computer can be told to support the model. Small models of parts of the academy must come together in large models of the entire academy before the different roles can effectively communicate through empowering software. The beginnings of these models have been sketched and case studies of the impact of automation of the models have been provided. The reader must now decide how to influence the direction of this evolving modeling and computerization activity

Figure 52: "Exercises and Answers". The stick figure is pondering an answer to a question.

Exercises and Answers

For this chapter of the book:

- The reader should attempt answers before reading the author's sketch of an answer.
- True-false answers require simple recall of the presentation in the book.
- Knowledge essays involve further recall of material from the book and perhaps some analysis.
- Doing essays require creativity.

This chapter contains exercises and answers. For true-false statements, the answer is given here, and if the answer is false, then the rewording that would make the statement true is offered. For the knowledge and doing essay questions, a brief answer is provided. The essay questions do not have yes-no answers and various different answers might be equally correct. The question is presented in italics and the answer in normal font. This chapter is organized so as to reflect the relevant section of the book.

Learning and Courseware

Learning and Pedagogy

True or False
At the simplest level, Bloom's Taxonomy identifies analysis and at the highest level it identifies evaluation. False. At the simplest level, Bloom's Taxonomy identifies recall and at the highest level it identifies evaluation.

Knowledge Essay
What does "learning by doing" mean? Learning by doing requires the student to be actively engaged in some meaningful constructive task and to learn in the course of making progress on that task. This is particularly different from learning by rote memory.

Doing Essays
Various cognitive learning taxonomies, such as the one called Bloom's have been constructed. Present your own version of a two-category cognitive learning taxonomy. *A simplified taxonomy divides learning into understanding what one has been told versus developing new insights by doing something in the world. This might roughly correspond to the Bloom taxonomy in that understanding alone would relate to knowledge and comprehension (the two lowest levels of the Bloom taxonomy) whereas new insights by doing would correspond to the highest levels of Bloom's Taxonomy, namely the synthesis and evaluation levels.*

Courseware Types

True or False

1. *An intelligent tutoring system contains exactly two models, one of the student and one of pedagogy.* False. An intelligent tutoring system contains at least three models, one of the student, one of pedagogy, and one of the domain.

2. *A meta-analysis may look at the result of one classroom experiment and determine the general conclusions.* False. A meta-analysis must look at the result of many classroom experiments before determining general conclusions.

3. *Virtual reality systems give users a sense of being in a real world situation when in fact they are not.* True

Knowledge Essays
Under what circumstances might paper be a better medium than the computer for delivery of educational material? An experiment was done with students learning from a paper book or an electronic book. For questions about the overall understanding of the book, those students who used the paper book did better than those who used the electronic book. Paper is better for understanding tasks, when the student must appreciate the full complexity of the material rather than just answer one specific question about a small part of the content. People are comfortable with paper.

Doing Essays

1. *Say that you want to use a combination of paper, interactive multiple-choice quizzes, and computer animations to teach a subject. What subject would you chose and why?* Anatomy might be a good subject to teach in the indicated way. Students could read descriptions of the characteristics of the anatomical parts. Quizzes could ask students questions like: "the arm is connected to a) the leg, b) the head, or c) the torso". Computer animations could show the parts of the body in action. For instance, the arm could be shown throwing a ball as a motion that relates to the torso as well as the connection of the hand to the ball.

2. *If you were to design an intelligent virtual reality tutoring system, what high level components would your system include and how would those components interact with one another?* In an intelligent virtual reality tutoring system, various high level components are required. The intelligent part of the system would contain the typical domain module, pedagogy module, and student module. Additionally for the virtual reality component one needs to have detailed models of the domain related to computer programs that can simulate the models and furthermore to render these simulations in understandable visual ways. Given that the user interacts with a virtual reality system, the system must have a sophisticated student model that anticipates and understands the input of the student and responds appropriately. While this is true of the responses to typical questions, such as multiple-choice questions, for the virtual reality simulation to seem meaningful it might face additional challenges of timing and realism.

3. *When a student starts to use an intelligent tutoring system, how can the system know what the student already knows in order that it can best guide the student?* The system could ask the student questions and develop a model of the student from that source. During a given course the computer can observe the student's behavior and infer attributes of the student. Ultimately, if the system were part of an integrated educational system that tracked students through various courses throughout their life, then the system could refer to the previous records of the student to understand what the student had learned and in what ways.

4. *Given that developing an intelligent tutoring system is expensive, what factors influence the decision as to whether or not to develop an intelligent tutor for a particular topic?* An intelligent tutoring system is only cost-effective when the revenues or other rewards generated by students using the system are greater than the costs in making and using the system. For instance, if millions of students were to use the system and would learn as well as when taught face-to-face by a human, then one could justify spending millions to build and deploy the intelligent tutoring system. Alternately, the few people who would use the system may be somehow in very special situations that merit great investment. For instance, the American military spends millions of dollars to develop intelligent tutoring systems that train people on responding to disasters on advanced weapons systems.

Courseware Production

True or False

1. *Teachers should NOT be expected to each produce their own courseware unassisted.* True

2. *Frequent involvement with end users is necessary for quality courseware production.* True.

3. *In the British state-funded learning technology efforts, academics focused on efficiency.* False. In the British state-funded courseware efforts, academics focused on quality and preferred to not consider efficiency.

4. *The creator organizational structure is the most effective in university courseware development projects.* False. The creator organizational structure does not provide enough organizational support to be effective.

Knowledge Essays

1. *Academics have traditionally treated courseware production like a cottage industry but that is changing. One early step is the creation of training facilities for faculty. What other steps might be taken?* Because faculty tends not to have experience with courseware authoring, they need training before they can contribute to courseware production. For books, a faculty member who wrote a dissertation already has experience. Furthermore, courseware involves more types of skill than book authoring. To support courseware production the university might make a clear commitment of resources to the development and maintenance of courseware. A well-funded organization within the university is created that has some authority in relationships with other support units and faculty. This would be the integrator model described in the book.

2. *The independent review of the British Teaching and Learning Technology Program suggested that funding go to the market and not to the supplier. What does this mean and why would this be the recommendation?* The recommendation was that students be able to select among those options, which are useful for them rather than schools themselves deciding what was best for students. In this way, the system might respond more closely to the needs of students than it would when only the schools decide what is best.

Doing Essays

1. *How would you organize a virtual courseware production operation as part of a university?* I would need a clear argument that we had enough expected return on our courseware to merit investment. I don't believe that a slipshod effort would do and a big effort requires a big audience. Then I would encourage budget-centered management, while also assuring a central commitment.

2. *Computers can represent models of reality and make these models come to life for students in an effort to teach the student about the models. What are the limiting factors in getting more of these models successfully incorporated into computers and delivered to students?* One limit is the high cost of developing the systems. Almost all aspects of these systems are costly to prepare. The domain knowledge is difficult to formalize and the multimedia presentations are difficult to make engrossing.

Teaching and Classrooms

Groupware

True or False
Mechanistic groupware focuses on supporting unstructured browsing. False. Mechanistic groupware specifies roles for people and directs their execution of the roles.

Knowledge Essay
Describe the four categories of groupware in terms of space and time sameness and give an example application of each. Same-time, same-place groupware would be something like a two-person, educational Nintendo game that two people would play at the same time in the same room. Same-time, different place groupware would be like audiovideoconferencing across the Internet. Different-time, same place would be like a physical library system, and different time, different place is illustrated by email.

Communication Channels

True or False

1. *Group hypertext for classroom learning was first used in the early 1990s.* False. Group hypertext for classroom learning was used much earlier than the 1990s.

2. *When comparing various channels of communication in the virtual classroom, the conclusion is consistently that video connections are the best for all kinds of learning.* False. When comparing various channels of communication in the virtual classroom, the conclusion is that some channels are appropriate for some kinds of learning and other channels are appropriate for other kinds of learning.

Knowledge Essays

1. *How are the guidelines for managing classroom videoconferences different from the guidelines for managing face-to-face class?* The guidelines for managing classroom videoconferencing are remarkably similar to the guidelines for managing face-to-face classrooms, except that in videoconferences one must pay special attention to the physical isolation of some individuals from others and attempt to help them feel connected. As senses of physical location are distorted in videoconferences, one must pay particular attention to using eyes, gestures, and more generally instructions to invite various people to interact.

2. *Compare and contrast a) group hypertext in which students add comments to an evolving document and b) classroom, electronic bulletin boards?* With classroom group hypertext, one is typically working from an established body of work (the document). The classroom, electronic bulletin board is normally only an archive of email and does not have a pre-planned infrastructure. The bulletin board thus lends itself more to an interaction among the participants, whereas the hypertext is better suited for guiding students in a certain topical direction.

Doing Essays
The multiple channels, virtual classroom experiment began to develop a mapping between media types and learning objectives. What mapping generalizations might you infer from the results of such experiments? Rich, multimedia communications support learning complex abstractions.

Simpler learning objectives may be practically handled with leaner, single media communications.

Asynchronous Classroom

True or False

1. *An asynchronous classroom does not require students to meet at any particular time.* True

2. *The trademarked Virtual Classroom was developed at New Jersey Institute of Technology and has been used for years in teaching full courses.* True

3. *Students felt they learned less from Virtual Classroom courses than from traditional courses.* False. Students felt they learned more or about the same from Virtual Classroom courses as from traditional courses.

4. *The costs to teachers for courses with more than 30 students are less with the Virtual Classroom than with a traditional class.* False. The costs to teachers for courses with more than 30 students are greater with the Virtual Classroom than with traditional classrooms.

Knowledge Essay
What were the strengths and weaknesses of the quantitative study done in the California State University Northridge Sociology course? Weaknesses included that all students were essentially in a position to go to class on some Saturdays. These were not students who truly had some great opportunity cost that prevented them from going to a room at Cal. State Northridge, USA. Also, interaction was strongly encouraged and required in the online class. We get no indication that interaction was systematically required in the face-to-face groups. Thus as is usual with such experiments there are too many variables that are different from what other people might experience for us to be able to draw firm conclusions from the study as to the impact for other classes in general.

Doing Essay
Would you use opportunity cost in assessing whether the virtual classroom method of teaching was better or worse than the alternatives? In assessing the course success one should use more than the traditional grades in the course or the student's perception of the effectiveness of the teacher. The salient factor missing from many academic reports of virtual classroom effectiveness is the opportunity cost to the student. In assessing a virtual classroom one should ask what students would miss this education if they could not participate in virtual mode.

Studio Course

True of False

1. *A Studio Course combines lectures, recitations, and labs.* True

2. *Students work alone at home and have no face-to-face meetings in a Studio Course.* False. Students attend multiple, weekly face-to-face meetings in a Studio Course.

3. *The Rensselear Polytechnic Studio courses have shown reduction in school costs and unchanged quality of learning.* False. The Rensselear Polytechnic Studio courses have shown reduction in school costs and improved learning at the same time.

Knowledge Essay

1. *In what ways does the Studio Course combine synchronous and asynchronous modalities?* The Studio Course encourages synchronous student-teacher interaction in real-time. At the same time it includes asynchronous features such as email and testing done to each individual's schedule.

2. *Why does the New Jersey Institute of Technology Virtual Classroom require greater teacher costs per student, while the Rensselaer Studio Physics Course reduces teacher costs per student?* NJIT's system required the teacher to interact with each student on email. The RPI system encouraged students to interact with one another and to use courseware. One should note that RPI assumes students are on campus and coming to meetings twice a week. NJIT wants students to be able to participate regardless of location.

Doing Essay

The studio course method has been shown to work well in physics. In what other disciplines do you think it would work well and in what disciplines would it not work and why? The studio course method has been shown to work well in physics and might work well in certain other disciplines. To the extent that the courseware is a valuable part of the classroom, disciplines without such courseware would be less suited. For instance, a philosophy course has less courseware available than a physics course and would thus be less likely to be successful with the studio course approach. The studio course typically involves a laboratory but only laboratory courses in which courseware exists for some labs would be appropriate.

Efficiency and Group Roles

True or False

1. *If roles in a group can be explicitly defined, then the computer can support the operation of student groups in which group members have distinct roles.* True

2. *Efficiency of a virtual classroom game system is based on the ratio of student-student interactions to student-teacher interactions.* True

Do Essays

1. Suggest how statistical process control might be applied in a virtual classroom to increase teacher efficiency while maintaining effectiveness. Statistical process control is a method for studying patterns across transactions and detecting those transactions that are likely to be beneath the quality threshold. Thus in the case of a virtual classroom, the teacher might use statistical process control to detect those student transactions that might be flawed. For instance, if a student x is grading another student y and gives a very different grade from what student z gives to student y, then the teacher might expect that either the grade given by x or by z is flawed. The teacher would not have to check all transactions but only those that the process control mechanism highlighted.

2. *Describe a course topic and a group of students such that detailed roles could be defined, the computer could manage the roles, and the students would learn by working together as a group with each a distinct role.* For various course topics, a group of students could have each specific roles and the computer could manage the roles. For instance, if we are to teach nurses how to work with a certain patient, then we could have nurses assume

different roles of the health care setting including that of the patient. The computer could know about the role responsibilities and messages that should go from role to role.

Administering Schools

History

True or False

1. *Medieval universities had large physical plants and bureaucracies.* False. Medieval universities often had no buildings and minimal administration, as professors practiced from the street and collected student fees directly.

2. *Seventeenth century American education was driven by scientific concerns.* False. Seventeenth century American education was driven by religious concerns.

3. *The competition between educational organizations teaching secular versus religious content with the monitorial method led to the first government involvement in education in England.* True

Knowledge Essays

1. *What is the purpose of education in society most broadly speaking?* The purpose of education is to perpetuate the society that provides the education. This society could be predominantly concerned about its religious values and have education be primarily about its religion. Or the concern could be political, scientific, or otherwise.

2. *Schools today often employ teaching assistants in the classroom. Compare and contrast this situation to that of the monitorial method.* The monitorial method had senior students teach junior students. This is very similar to what happens with teaching assistants at universities.

Do Essays

1. *To the extent that lecture and memorization dominated teaching in the medieval university, to what extent do modern universities teach differently and why?* Lecture and memorization dominated teaching in the medieval university and often seem to dominate it today too. The reasons for this lack of progress may be the economics of education. It is inexpensive for the teacher to lecture to large numbers of students in a classroom but more costly for the teacher to manage a class in which students experience individualized, meaningful interaction.

2. *Do people across different historical periods fear the information explosion is most severe for them?* Yes, and that anxiety is certainly present now. Fortunately, the same tools that lead to the information explosion can at times help manage that explosion. The World Wide Web is a good example of a tool that supports the information explosion but education across the Web could help people develop models of the new information that would make it seem less of an explosion.

Delivering

True or False
Budget-centered management means that the central administration of the university takes all responsibility for management. False. Budget-centered management means that each unit takes responsibility for its own management.

Knowledge Essays

1. *What are the differences in teaching loads in community colleges versus research universities and why?* Community college teachers are in the classroom much of the workweek, whereas research university professors may spend less than half of their time in classroom-related activities. This is because the research university faculties are expected to spend much of their time engaged in research.

2. *What is budget centered management and what forces work against its success?* In budget-centered management, units within an organization each have their own budgets and must earn enough revenue to cover their costs. Furthermore a unit that earns above its costs can reinvest its profit in growth of the unit. In an organization where units that are not economically successful but are nevertheless politically powerful, budget centered management might be difficult.

Doing Essays

1. *Why is responsibility-centered management well suited to a virtual educational organization?* The virtual organization has massive amounts of information on the computer. When the model of the organization is precise and gains can be related to performance and performers can spend their own gains, then rules can be formalized that support the organization.

2. *Illustrate how information technology applications in education support the unbundling of the product.* In a classroom, one person or program might guide the students through some educational material, while another person or program might assess student progress. Students might take a course at one school and another course at a different school at the same time and independently of geographic considerations.

Systems

True or False

1. *A large university typically employs a few dozen programmers whose job is to develop or tailor software for the school.* False. A large university typically employs hundreds of programmers whose job is to develop or tailor software for the school.

2. *Authorization is an important function for determining who has permission to do what on the system and is a significantly different issue from security.* True.

Knowledge Essays

1. *What advantages could accrue to the world, if an education information system architecture were standardized?* Users could find components more reliably at cheaper prices. Components of one system could be exchanged with components of another system more easily and thus increase the overall functionality available to the user.

2. *Briefly describe the high-level structure, function model of an education information system.* The high-level structure, function model of an education information system has students interacting with teachers and teaching assistants through a student management module. Other support structures feed into this student management, which is also overseen by a central administration module.

Quality Control

True or False
No universities have been ISO 9000 certified. False. The University of Wolverhampton was ISO 9000 certified.

Knowledge Essays
What is ISO 9000? ISO 9000 is a standard of the International Standards Organization that describes the processes an organization should follow so as to assure that it operates in a quality way.

Doing Essays

1. *If quality management is basically a challenge of matching objectives to what the documentation of the organization shows was achieved, then how might an extensive electronic information system make it easier for someone to determine whether or not an organization operates in a quality way?* An extensive electronic information system makes it easier for someone to determine whether or not an organization operates in a quality way. If the goals of the organization and the signs of progress to those goals are in the form of documents that are archived on the Web, then it should be a relatively simple matter to connect goals and signs of progress on the Web. Then people in the organization and outside should be able to readily check whether quality is maintained.

2. *How might certification as being ISO 9000 compliant be more relevant to virtual educational organizations than traditional school accreditation?* Traditional accrediters specify independently of the school what the school goals should be and these criteria are typically traditional. ISO 9000 on the other hand applies equally to many organizations and emphasizes only the process. In this way it might be more flexible and help virtual educational organizations get certified as quality compliant. Also ISO 9000 is recognized around the world, whereas other school accreditation organizations are normally geographically local in their audience.

New Marketing Opportunities

Doing Essays

Suggest aspects of a marketing module that might be added to the structure/function model of an education information system. The marketing module of an education information system must present a good image of the school to select audiences, and this entails showing how the curriculum will lead to satisfactory results for enrollees. The marketing system would also track alumni and enroll their support in recruiting new students. The marketing module would connect to the quality control module for evidence of school success that could be advertised.

Employees

Doing Exercises:

1. *Describe a strategy for education for employees in some corporation of your choice such that the information superhighway is used as much as possible.* I would connect the normal corporate information system to the educational one. Thus employee or manager reports of needs for increased competency could be directly linked to the educational system. Second, I would look for corporate educational tools that could harmonize as

much as possible with the existing infrastructure of the company. Then I would relate the achievement tests of the education to the needs of the company.

2. *In working with a company, might your university educate the employees of the company and the customers of the company simultaneously? What would be the pros and cons to a joint strategy for employees and customers?* The joint strategy could have the advantage of economies of scale and also of bringing employees more directly in touch with customers. However, barriers include that customers may have very different tool sets and work styles than employees and thus not want to be served by the same educational tools or methods. The customers' educational needs may be so different from the employees that only a small subset of employees and customers have much to share – this would have to be decided on a case-by-case basis.

Brokers

True or False

The National Technological University focuses on course offerings to the general public rather than targeting companies whose employees would enroll. False. The National Technological University focuses on course offerings to employees of companies rather than targeting the general public.

Knowledge exercises:

1. *What internal tensions has the Washington Governors University (WGU) faced?* The WGU faces competition from its own member state educational institutions. Those institutions have a legacy of autonomy that may leave them feeling threatened by the WGU.

2. *Describe the mechanisms of an organization that connects schools with companies and illustrate this mechanism with details from the National Technological University.* An organization that connects schools with companies makes contracts with schools and with companies to deliver education from the schools to the companies. NTU has been doing this since 1984 largely via interactive satellite audiovideo broadcasts. In the NTU case the lectures are the standard university lectures given simultaneously to students in the lecture room and to students seated in some downlink satellite site at a company.

3. *What are the similarities between Jones International University and the International School of Information Management as they illustrate the operations of a virtual educational organization that connects teachers and students?* The Jones International University and the International School of Information Management illustrate the operations of a virtual educational organization that connects teachers and students. Both International University and ISIM recruit students from the general public and faculty from other organizations. Both rely extensively on the Internet for virtual classrooms that are largely asynchronous discussion sites.

4. *What are characteristics of a self-organizing catalog and how does the Globewide Network Academy manifest those properties?* A self-organizing catalog is built by individuals or organizations contributing catalog entries through a software system that guides them in making their contribution and automatically organizes the submitted information. The catalog is also made accessible to others through software tools. The Globewide Network Academy has created such a self-organizing catalog.

5. *In what way is a franchiser a broker. Illustrate with the case of the company, Fourth R.* A franchiser grants a license to other organizations to operate with marketing and other

benefits from the licenser. To the extent that the franchisee is engaged in educational activity, the franchiser is a kind of broker – it coordinates the work across franchisees. The Fourth R has about 100 franchisees that help schools provide information technology education to their students. Each Fourth R store makes contracts with schools and contracts with teachers to support the schools in the specialty activity of information technology education.

Doing essays:
How would you see yourself creating a private, global virtual educational broker that would only market directly to students and that would compete effectively with state-funded organizations. Competing against the state-funded organizations is difficult. For certain very specialized or high demand topics one could hope to recruit faculty that had a special reputation and attracted certain students in the same sense that private, traditional schools do this now. Alternately, to flourish the virtual school could intend to tailor the offerings to corporate needs in ways that public schools tend not to do.

Publishers

True or False:
The Ziff Davis Net University charged students only a few dollars a month for unlimited course access. True.

Knowledge exercises:

1. *Describe the role of publishers in virtual education.* Publishers have both copyrights on valuable educational material and have expertise in guiding to market new educational products.

2. W*hy might McGraw-Hill's Continuing Professional Education division target Certified Public Accountants?* McGraw-Hill's Continuing Professional Education division targets Certified Public Accountants because Certified Public Accountants need to continually get re-certified through continuing education.

3. *How did the private, for-profit ZDUNet University manage to prosper while charging students less than $5 per month for unlimited access?* The benefit to ZDUNet was not necessarily the student fee alone but also the derivative benefits. Students buy Ziff Davis products in order to maximally benefit from the courses.

Doing Essay
How would you have extended the range of ZDUNet services to merit different per month costs? I would extend the range of ZDUNet services. I would offer students an opportunity to pay more and to get more individualized interaction with the authors and teaching assistants. Another direction to pursue is the combining of sequences of offerings from ZDUNet into certificate programs.

Conclusion

True or False
Friction-free capitalism connects buyers and sellers through a middleman. False. Friction-free capitalism removes the middleman.

Knowledge essay

1. *How does the mapping among tools, people, and problems create a framework for dialectic?* As tools change, the best mapping of a people to their tools to serve their educational needs may change. The change needs to occur to resolve the tension that the strained, old mapping has caused. But change will continue, and new mappings will be necessary. This continual tension introduced by change and resolved by new mappings is dialectic.

2. *Give an example of the application of friction-free capitalism to education.* A teacher can advertise a course on the Web and accept students directly into the teacher's class. Of course, students have to want this education independently of the many benefits that a school, operating in the middle, might otherwise bring.

Doing essays

1. *Propose a discipline for your own virtual college and explain why this choice would help you market.* I would choose any discipline in which professionals need to be continually re-certified. Examples include health care professionals and K-12 teachers.

2. *Make your own predictions for five and thirty years forward.* Within five years, publicly funded education will have increasingly crossed state boundaries and teachers and students will interact across vast distances. Courseware may have become so popular thirty years hence that it has replaced the book and television as the media object of choice for students.

3. *Describe one popular mapping of people, tools, and problems. Then propose a different mapping to which you think these people will move in the future.* A common mapping for part-time graduate students in computer science who work is to commute to the neighborhood university for evening lectures a few times a week. For work- or home-bound students, this mapping could become inferior to the mapping by which they participate in virtual classrooms.

**Figure 53:
References to
further reading.**

References

Adams, W.H., "Faculty Load" *Improving College and University Teaching* 24, 4 (1976), pp. 215–218.

Annis, P., *Use of telephones and computers in the classroom at Boston University* (1992) (This work was distributed to various Internet newsgroups in 1992, copy was obtainable from the author at email address annis@crca.bu.edu.)

AICC *Aviation Industry Computer-Based Training Committee* (2000) http://www.aicc.org/

Avner, A., "Production of Computer-Based Instructional Materials" *Issues in Instructional Systems Development*, ed. H.F. O'Neil, Jr., Academic Press: New York, (1979) pp. 133–180.

Ballatyne, C., "Multiple Choice Tests" Murdoch University (2000) http://cleo.murdoch.edu.au/evaluation/pubs/mcq/mctests.html.

Bates, A.W., *Technology, Open Learning and Distance Education*, London/New York: Routledge, Actions Model (1995), ISBN: 0-415-11682-1.

Bennett, R.E., "Reinventing Assessment: Speculations on the Future of Large-Scale Educational Testing" *Educational Testing Service* (2000), http://www.ets.org/research/textonly/pic/reinvsec2.html

Berners-Lee, T.; Cailliau, R.; Luotonen, A.; Nielsen, N.F. and Secret, A. "The World Wide Web" *Communications of the ACM*, 37, 8 (1994) pp. 76–82.

Bibby, P., *An Academic Accounting Model for Community Colleges* (1983) Ph.D. University of Florida.

Black, J., "Tools of the trade" *cnet news* http://www.news.com/SpecialFeatures/ 0,5,8360,00.html, Feb. 28, (1997).

Blaye, A.; Light, P.H.; Joiner, R. and Sheldon, S. "Joint planning and problem solving on a computer-based task" *British Journal of Developmental Psychology, 9*, (1991) pp. 471–483.

Bloom, B.S., editor *Taxonomy of Educational Objectives Handbook 1: Cognitive Domain*, David McKay Company: New York (1956).

Boehm, E., "International School of Information Management" (2000) *http://www.isimu.edu/*.

Bonk, C.J. and King, K.S., editors "Electronic Collaborators – Learner-Centered Technologies for Literacy, Apprenticeship and Discourse" Lawrence Erlbaum Associates: Mahwah, New Jersey (1998).

Bowen, H., *The Costs of Higher Education: How Much Do Colleges and Universities Spend per Student and How Much Should They Spend?* San Francisco, Jossey-Bass (1980).

Boyd, W., *The History of Western Education*, Adam & Charles Black: London (1968).

Brown, J.S. and Burton, R., "Diagnostic Models for Procedural Bugs in Mathematical Skills" *Cognitive Science* 2, (1978) pp. 155–192.

Carr, S., "For Sale to the Highest Bidders: 3 Seats in a Course at Georgetown U." also available at http://chronicle.com/free/2000/01/2000011401t.htm, *Chronicle of Higher Education* (January 14 2000).

Cartwright, P., "Teaching with Dynamic Technologies: Part I" *Change Magazine* Nov/Dec, also at http://contract.kent.edu/change/articles/novdec93.html (1993).

CEN TC/251 "Healthcare Information System Architecture" *CEN/TC 251 WG1* http://www.centc251.org/ (2000).

Cerny, J., "Questioning Menu" at http://www.hcc.hawaii.edu/hccinfo/facdev/questionmenu.html (1997).

Chen, C. and Rada, R., 'Interacting with hypertext: A meta-analysis of experimental studies" *Human-Computer Interaction*, 11, 2 (1996) pp. 125–156.

Chesterton, G.K., *All I Survey: a book of essays,* Dodd, Mead & Company: New York (1933).

Cleverley, J., *The Schooling of China: tradition and modernity in Chinese education* Allen & Unwin: North Sydney, Australia (1991).

Collis, B. and DeBoer, W.F., "Faculty level; self-authored TeLeTOP© system and resources": Case studies at University of Twente, NL. *Interactive Learning Environments*, 7 (2/3) (2000).

Collis, B. & Moonen, J., "Leadership for transition: Moving from the special project to systemwide integration with computers in education" in G. Kearsley & W. Lynch (Eds.) *Educational technology: Leadership perspectives* (pp. 113-136). Englewood Cliffs, NJ: Educational Technology Press. (1994).

Connect "CONNECT On-line" from Impresso Incorporated at *http://cool.connectinc.com/cool/education.html* (2000).

Coopers & Lybrand, London Institute of Education, and Tavistock Institute "Evaluation of the Teaching and Learning Technology Programme (TLTP*)" Active Learning,* 5, (1996) pp. 60–63.

Corvetta, A.G.; Pomponio, A.; Salvi, M.. and Luchetti, M., "Teaching Medicine Using Hypertext: Three Years of Experience at the Ancona Medical School" *Artificial Intelligence in Medicine*, 3, pp. 203–209 (1991).

Daniel, J., *Mega-Universities and Knowledge Media: Technology Strategies for Higher Education*, Kogan Page Limited: London, England (1998).

DeBoer, W.F. and Collis, B., "The TeLeTOP Implementation Model: Version 1 and Validation" *Interactive Learning Environments*, 7 2/3 (2000).

DETC "What is Distance Education?" *http://www.detc.org/* Distance Education and Training Council, 1601 18th Street, N.W., Washington, D.C. (2000).

Diaz, L., "PathMAC: An Alternative Approach to Medical School Education at Cornell School of Medicine" in *Hypertext/Hypermedia Handbook*, E. Berk and J. Devlin (eds.), McGraw-Hill: New York (1991) pp. 488–492

Dillenbourg, M.; Baker, A.; Blaye and O'Malley, C., "The evolution of Research on Collaborative Learning" in Spada and Reimann (eds), *Learning in Humans and Machines* also at http://tecfa.unige.ch/tecfa-people/dillenbourg.html (1996).

Dillman, D.; James, C.; Salant, P.; and Warner, P.; *What the Public Wants from Higher Education: Work Force Implications from a 1995 National Survey,* Social & Economic Sciences Research Center, Washington State University, Pullman, WA. (1995).

Diversity University *Diversity University Web Gateway*, http://moo.du.org/ (2000).

DLRN "Bloom's Taxonomy" Chapter 5 of WestEd *Technology Resource Guide* http://www.wested.org/edtech/blooms.html (1997).

Duderstadt, J., "The Modern University" at *http://www.professionals.com/ ~chepc/ct_1095/ctov1_1095.html* (1995).

Duggan, S., "A Student's Textbook in the History of Education", Appleton-Century: New York (1936) Edelson, D.C., Pea, R.D. and Gomez, L. "Constructivism in the collaboratory," *in Constructivist LearningEnvironments: Case studies in instructional design*, edited B. G. Wilson, Educational Technology Publications: Englewood Cliffs, NJ (1995).

Egido, C., "Videoconferencing as a technology to support group work: a review of its failure" *Second Conference on Computer-Supported Cooperative Work: CSCW '88*, Association of Computing Machinery: New York (1988) pp. 13–24.

Engelbart, D.C. and English, W.K., "A Research Center for Augmenting Human Intellect" *American Federation of Information Processing Societies, Conference Proceedings of the Fall Joint Computer Conference, Volume 33*, Thompson Book Company, Washington, D.C. (1968) pp. 395–410.

FairTest *Computerized Testing: More Questions Than Answers*, The National Center for Fair and Open Testing, http://www.fairtest.org/facts/computer.htm (2000).

Farance, F. and Tonkel, J., *Learning Technology Systems Architecture (LTSA) Specification*, http://www.edutool.com/ltsa/ (2000).

Forsyth, R. and Rada, R.,*Machine Learning: Expert Systems and Information Retrieval*, Ellis Horwood: London (1986).

Fortune Magazine "Fortune 500 Ranked within Industries" *Fortune Magazine* http://www.pathfinder.com/fortune/fortune500/ (2000).

Fourth, R., "The Fourth R Home Page" *http://www.fourthr.com/* (2000).

Fryer, R., "Computerworld's Third Annual Top Techno-MBA Survey" *ComputerWorld*, http://www.computerworld.com/home/print.nsf/all/990927C35A (Sept. 27 1999).

Fullan, M., *The meaning of educational change*, New York: Teachers College Press (1991).

Gates, B., *The Road Ahead* http://www.penguin.com/RoadAhead/book/cap.html, Penguin Books (1996).

Gates, B. *Business @ the Speed of Thought*, http://www.speed-of-thought.com/index_home.html from Warner Books: http://www.twbookmark.com/ (1999)

Gay, G. and Lentini, M., "Use of Communication Resources in a Networked Collaborative Design Environment" *Journal of Computer Mediated Communication*, vol. 1, no. 1, at; http://www.ascuse.org/jcmc/vol1/issue1/IMG_IL_MC/ResourceUse.html (1999).

Glendenning, P., "Governor Will Dedicate Surplus Funds to Make Long-term Investments in Maryland's Future" announced December 16, 1999 at University of Maryland, Baltimore County and archived at: http://www.gov.state.md.us/gov/press/1999/dec/html/highered.html, (1999).

GNA, *Globewide Network Academy* http://www.gnacademy.org/ (2000).

Green, K., *The 1999 National Survey of Information Technology in Higher Education* http://www.campuscomputing.net/ (1999).

GTE "Continue Your Professional Development, Courses Now Offered on the Intranet" *GTE Telephone Operations Employee Bulletin*, Volume 9, Issue 054, Published Electronically by Telephone Operations Headquarters Public Affairs, Stamford, Conn. (February 13 1997).

Hall, J., and Brown, M., *Online Bibliographic Databases*, ASLIB, London (1983).

Harrison, M.J., "Quality Policy University of Wolverhampton: Profile 1995-96" *http://www.wlv.ac.uk/www/university/profile/quality.html* (1996).

Hayes, F., "The Groupware Dilemma" *UnixWorld*, 9, 2, (1992) pp. 46–50.

Haynie, W.J., "Effects of Multiple-Choice and Short-Answer Tests on Delayed Retention Learning" *Journal of Technology Education*, Vol. 6, No. 1 (1994)

Hiltz, S.R., "Teaching in a Virtual Classroom" *1995 International Conference on Computer Assisted Instruction ICCAI'95*, March 7–10, 1995 National Chiao Tung University, Hsinchu, Taiwan, also available at: http://it.njit.edu/njIT/Department/CCCC/VC/Papers/Teaching.html

Hodas, S., "Technology Refusal and The Organizational Culture of Schools" in R. Kling (ed.), *Computerization and Controversy (2d ed.)* San Diego: Academic Press (1996) (1996).

Hopper, M., "*Courseware Projects in Advanced Educational Computing Environments*" Ph.D. Thesis Purdue University (1993) House, E.R., "*The Politics of Educational Innovation*". Los Angeles, CA: McCutchan Publications (1974).

Huff, C., and Finholt, T., (eds) "*Social Issues in Computing*" McGraw-Hill: New York (1994).

Huyink, D.S., and Westover C., *Iso 9000: Motivating the People, Mastering the Process, Achieving Registration*, Irwin Professional Publications (1994).

IMS "Defining the Internet Architecture for Learning" http://www.imsproject.org/ (2000)

ISO "International Organization for Standardization: ISO 9000" http://www.iso.ch (2000)

Isaacs, E.A., and Tang, J.C., "What video can and can't do for collaboration: a case study" *Proceedings of ACM Multimedia '93*, ACM Press: New York (1993), pp. 199–206 IUS (Indiana University Southeast) "Accreditation" *http://www.cs.ius.indiana.edu/bulletin/accred.htm* (2000).

Jense, G.J., and Kuijper, F., "Applying Virtual Environments to Training and Simulation" *Annual Meeting of the Applied Vision Association*, University of Bristol, England, (1993).

JIU *Jones International University*, http://www.jonesinternational.edu/ (2000).

Johansen, R., "User Approaches to Computer-Supported Teams" in *Technological Support for Work Group Collaborations*, M H Olson (ed), Lawrence Erlbaum Associates: Hillsdale, New Jersey (1989) pp. 1–32.

Johnson-Lenz, P. and Johnson-Lenz, T., "Post-mechanistic Groupware Primitives: Rhythms, Boundaries, and Containers" *International Journal of Man-Machine Studies*, 34, 3, (1991) pp. 385–418.

Jonassen, D.H., *Computers As Mindtools for Schools: Engaging Critical Thinking, 2nd edition*, Prentice Hall: Englewood Cliffs, NJ (2000).

Katz, R.N. (ed), *Dancing With the Devil: Information Technology and the New Competition in Higher Education*, Jossey-Bass Publishers: San Francisco, CA, (1999).

Katz-Stone, A., "Online Learning: University of Maryland Expects to make Money from UMUC Online.com" *Washington Business Journal* (January 21 2000), pp. 35–36.

Klavins, E., "COW, Conferencing on the Web" from *http://thecity.sfsu.edu/ COW2/* (2000).

Krol, E., *The Whole Internet: User's Guide and Catalog*, O'Reilly & Associates: Sebastopol, California (1992).

Kumar, V., "Computer-Supported Collaborative Learning: Issues for Research" http://www.cs.usask.ca/grads/vsk719/academic/890/project2/project2.html (1996),

Landow, G.P., "Hypertext and collaborative work: The example of Intermedia" in *Intellectual Teamwork: Social Foundations of Cooperative Work*, Jolene Galegher, Robert Kraut and Carmen Egido (eds), Lawrence Erlbaum Associates: Hillsdale, New Jersey (1990) pp. 407–428.

Lawrence, G. and Service, A. (eds), *Quantitative Approaches to Higher Education Management: Potential, Limits, and Challenges*, American Association for Higher Education (1977).

Lenzner, R., and Johnson, S.S., "Seeing things as they really are" at *http://www.forbes.com/forbes/97/0310/5905122a.htm* Forbes Magazine (March 10 1997).

Liu, D., *Teaching Chemistry on the Internet: a Qualitative Study*, Ph.D. Thesis at University of Nebraska at Lincoln, also available at http://www.cci.unl.edu/ CVs/Dissertations/liuDiss.html, (1996).

LTSC "Learning Technologies Standards Committee" *Institute of Electrical and Electronic Engineers*, http://ltsc.ieee.org/ (2000).

Magna Publications "Using Technology to Recruit" Magna Publications, Inc.: Madison, Wisconsin, http://www.magnapubs.com/R_R/using3.5.htm (2000).

Massy, W. and Zemsky, R., "Using Information Technology to Enhance Academic Productivity"*http://www.educom.edu/program/nlii/keydocs/massy.html*, Educomreg., Interuniversity Communications Council (1995).

McDonough, D., Strivens, J. and Rada, R., "University Courseware Development: Differences between Computer-Based Teaching Users and Non-Users" *Computers and Education*, 23, 3, (1994) pp. 211–220.

McGraw-Hill "McGraw-Hill Online Learning" *http://www.mhonlinelearning.com/* (2000).

Merriam Webster Dictionary Merriam-Webster, Inc. http://www.m-w.com/dictionary.htm (2000).

Mizoguchi, R., Sinitsa, K. and Ikeda, M., "Task Ontology Design for Intelligent Educational/Training Systems" *ITS'96 Workshop on Architectures and Methods for Designing Cost-Effective and Reusable ITSs*, Montreal (June 10 1996) http://advlearn.lrdc.pitt.edu/its-arch/papers/mizoguchi.html.

Mulhern, J., *A History of Education*, Ronald Press, New York (1959).

Murray, T. "Authoring Intelligent Tutoring Systems: Analysis of the state of the art" *International Journal of AI and Education*, vol. 10, no. 1 (1999).

NACTEL "National Advisory Coalition for Telecommunications Education and Learning" www.nactel.org, (2000).

National Center for Education *Statistics Statistical Analysis Report: Distance Education in Higher Education Institutions NCES 98-062*, US Government Printing Office, (1997).

National Committee of Inquiry into Higher Education "Evidence from the Computers in Teaching Initiative" *Active Learning* 5, (1996) pp. 64–70.

Nelson, K.R. and Scoby, J.L., "Implementing Decentralized Responsibility-Centered Management with Budget Restructuring and Cutting Edge Technologies", *EduCause98*, http://www.educause.edu/ir/library/html/cnc9858/cnc9858.html (1998).

Newpromise.com "Newpromise" www.newpromise.com (2000).

NGI "Internet Trends", Center for Next Generation Internet, http://www.ngi.org/trends.htm (2000).

NIST "Baldrige National Quality Program: 1999 Education Criteria for Educational Excellence" *National Institute of Standards and Technology*, at http://www.quality.nist.gov/docs/99_crit/99edcrit.doc (1999).

Noam, E. "Electronic Information and the Dim Future of the University" *Science*, 270, (Oct. 13 1995), pp. 247-249.

NovaNet "NovaNet Home Page" http://www.novanet.com/ (2000).

Novell "Education" http://www.novell.com/ (2000).

Novick, D. and Fickas, S. "Collaborative networked hypermedia education: lessons from the NERO project" *Computers and Education*, 24, (1995) pp. 157–162.

NRI "Brief History of NRI Schools" *http://nrischools..com/* (2000).

NTU *National Technological University*, http://www.ntu.edu/ (2000).

O'Malley, C. and Scanlon, E., "Computer supported collaborative learning: problem solving and distance education" *Computer Education 15* (1990) pp.127–136.

OPA (Office of Planning and Analysis) *Responsibility Center Management* Report of the Responsibility Center Management Working Committee, University of Minnesota, *http://www.opa.pres.umn.edu /specproj/rcm/rpt1 .htm* (1996).

Open University "What is the Open University?" *http://www.open.ac.uk/* (2000).

Oracle Corporation "Oracle Corporation Home Page"*http://www.oracle.com* (2000).

Orlikowski, W., "The Duality of Technology: Rethinking the Concept of Technology in Organizations" *Organization Science*, 3, 3 (1992) pp. 398–427.

Pace University "Associate of Telecommunications Degree" http://csis.pace.edu/nactel/ (2000).

Palloff, R. and Pratt, K., *Building Learning Communities in Cyberspace : Effective Strategies for the Online Classroom*, Jossey-Bass Publishers: San Francisco, CA, (1999).

Park, C., "Franchising Computers for The Fourth R" *Small Business Week* (March 20, 1997), pp. 40–41.

Petersons.com "Petersons.com: the Education Superstore" www.peterson.com, (2000).

Piaget, J., *Judgement and Reasoning in the Child*, Harcourt Brace: New York (1928).

QuestionMark "UC Irvine Utilizes Web-Based Tests for In-Class Learning" Question Mark Computing Limited, http://www.questionmark.com/casestudies/uc_irvine_utilizes_web.htm (2000).

Rada, R.; Keith, B.; Burgoine, M.; George, S. and Reid, D., "Collaborative Writing of Text and Hypertext" *Hypermedia*, 1(2) (1989), pp. 93–110.

Rada, R., *Hypertext: from Text to Expertext*, McGraw-Hill: London (1991).

Rada, R., "Hypertext and Paper: a Special Synergy", *International Journal of Information Management*, 11, (1991a), pp. 14–22.

Rada, R., and Murphy, C., "Searching versus Browsing in Hypertext" *Hypermedia*, 4, 1 (1992), pp. 1–30.

Rada, R., *Developing Educational Hypermedia: Coordination and Reuse*, Ablex Publishing: Norwood, New Jersy (1995a).

Rada, R., *Interactive Media*, Springer Verlag: New York (1995b).

ReverseAuction "Georgetown University Certificate in Multimedia" at http://www.reverseauction.com/ (2000).

Rice, R. and Shook, D.E., "Relationships of Job Categories and Organizational Levels to Use of Communication Channels, Including Electronic Mail: A Meta-Analysis and Extension" *Journal of Management Studies*, 27, 2 (1990), pp. 195–229.

Rodden, T., "A Survey of CSCW Systems" *Interacting with Computers*, 3, 2 (1991), pp. 319–353.

RPI "Studio Courses" Rensselaer Polytechnic Institute at *http://ciue.rpi.edu/studio/Studio.htm* (2000).

Russel, S. and Norvig, P., *Artificial Intelligence: A Modern Approach*, Prentice Hall: Englewood Cliffs, NJ (1995).

Russell, T.L.,*"The 'No Significant Difference' Phenomenon as reported in 248 Research Reports", Summaries, and Papers, Fourth Edition*, North Carolina State University, http://tenb.mta.ca/phenom/ nsd.txt (1997).

Schank, R., "Engines for Education" *http://www.ils.nwu.edu/~e_for_e/nodes/I-M-INTRO-ZOOMER-pg.html* (1997).

Schank, R., *"Dynamic Memory Revisited"* Cambridge Univ. Press: Cambridge, England, (2000).

Schutte, J., "Virtual Teaching in Higher Education: The New Intellectual Superhighway or Just Another Traffic Jam?" *http://www.csun.edu/sociology/virexp.htm* (1997).

SCT "Banner2000 Overview" *http://www.sctcorp.com/*, Systems and Computer Technology Incorporated, (2000).

Shackelford, R.L., "Educational Computing: Myths versus Methods – Why Computers Haven't Helped and What We Can Do about it," *Proceedings of the Conference on Computers and the Quality of Life*, The George Washington University: Washington, D.C., (1990), pp. 139–146

Shneiderman, B., "Engagement and construction: education strategies for the post-TV era" *Jr of Computing in Higher Education*, 4, 2 (1993), pp. 106–116.

Shneiderman, B., "Home Page" *http://www.cs.umd.edu/users/ben/index.html* (1997).

SmartPlanet *SmartPlanet.com – Live Long and Learn*, http://www.smartplanet.com/ (2000).

Snyder, J.M.., *An Investigation into the Factors that Encourage University Faculty to Use Information Technologies in their Teaching* Ph.D. Dissertation, University of Nebraska at Lincoln (1995).

Southwest Missouri State University "Master of Science in Computer Information Systems" *http://www.cis .masters.smsu.edu/*, (2000).

Stiles, R.; McCarthy, L.; Munro, A.; Pizzini, Q.; Johnson, L. and Rickel, J., "Virtual Environments for Shipboard Training" Printed in the *Proceedings of the Intelligent Ships Symposium*, American Society of Naval Engineers, Philadelphia, PA also available at http://vet.parl.com/~vet/iships/iships.html (Nov. 1996).

Storey, S. "ISO 9001 University" in *TQM in Higher Education* (1994), pp. 1–2.

Teare, R.; Davies, D. and Sanderlands, E., "*The Virtual University: An Action Paradigm and Process for Workplace Learning*" (1995), Cassell Academic: London, England, (1999).

Todd, P.; McKeen, J. and Gallupe, R.B., "The Evolution of IS Job Skills: A Content Analysis of IS Job Advertisements from 1970 to 1990" *MIS Quarterly: Volume 19, Number 1* (1995).

Turroff, M., "Designing a Virtual Classroom" *1995 International Conference on Computer Assisted Instruction ICCAI'95* March 7-10, 1995 National Chiao Tung University Hsinchu, Taiwan available at http://it.njit.edu/njIT/ Department/CCCC/VC/Papers/Design.html (1995).

UMUC "University of Maryland University College: Office of Institutional Planning" http://www.umuc.edu/ip/ (2000).

USDE (United States Department of Education) "Accreditation in the United States", Accrediting Agency Evaluation Branch, U.S. Department of Education, 600 Independence Avenue, S.W., Washington, D.C. (2000).

Van Marcke, K. et al. "Learner adaptivity in generic instructional strategies" *Proc. of AIED95* (1995) pp.323–333.

Vasandani, V. and Govindaraj, T., "Knowledge Organization in Intelligent Tutoring Systems for Problem Solving in Complex Dynamic Domains" *IEEE Transactions on Systems, Man, and Cybernetics, SMC-25*, and available at http://www.isye.gatech.edu/chmsr/T_Govindaraj/papers/knowledge.ps (1995).

Wenger, E. *Artificial intelligence and tutoring systems*, Morgan Kaufmann Publishers, California (1987).

Warren, K. and Rada, R., "Sustaining Computer-Mediated Communication in University Courses Through Computer Managed Messaging Systems" *Journal of Computer-Assisted Learning, Vol. 11 (1998) pp. 71–80*

WGU "Western Governors University" www.wgu.edu (2000).

Winograd, T and Flores, F., *Understanding Computers and Cognition: A New Foundation for Design*, Ablex; Norwood, New Jersey (1986).

Woodruff, M. and Mosby, J., "*A Brief Description of VideoConferencing*" http://www.kn.pacbell.com/wired/vidconf/description.html (1997).

Woolley, D.R., "PLATO: The Emergence of On-Line Community" *http://www.xxlink.nl/ plato1.htm*, (1994).

Xerox "Xerox Fact Book" *http://www.xerox.com/* (2000).

Zammuto, R., *Assessing Organizational Effectiveness*, State University of New York Press: Albany, New York (1982

Index